GOINGPUBLIC

GOINGPUBLIC

Christian Responsibility in a Divided America

Lawrence E. Adams

Brazos Press

A Division of Baker Book House Co
Grand Rapids, Michigan 49516

Published by Brazos Press
a division of Baker Book House Company
P.O. Box 6287, Grand Rapids, MI 49516-6287

Printed in the United States of America

Library of Congress Cataloging-in-Publication Data

Adams, Lawrence E., 1953–
    Going public : Christian responsibility in a divided America / Lawrence E.
Adams.
        p.   cm.
    Includes bibliographical references and index.
    ISBN 1-58743-030-4 (pbk.)
    1. Christianity and politics—United States. 2. Christianity and culture—
United States. I. Title.
BR526 .A32 2002
261.7′0973—dc21
                                           2001056600

For current information about all releases from Brazos Press, visit our web site:
http://www.brazospress.com

Contents

5

102527

Acknowledgments

Much of the work on this book was undertaken during a research fellowship at the University of Virginia, under the auspices of the Postmodernity Project (now known as the Institute for Advanced Studies in Culture). My appreciation to James Davison Hunter, director of the institute, for the support and infrastructure provided for this research. I would also like to thank my colleagues and former students from my years at North Park College in Chicago for providing a regular forum for the exchange of ideas and clarification of concepts—especially Professors Warren Wade, Dan deRoulet, David Nystrom, David Koehler, and David Gill. At Brazos Press, I am deeply grateful to Rodney Clapp and especially to Steve Ayers for their encouragement and enthusiasm for this project. I am also grateful to Drew Trotter and the staff of the Center for Christian Study in Charlottesville, Virginia, for providing other avenues for exploring the themes of this book. And above all, I could not have done this work or any other without the steadfast love and loyalty of my wife, Beth, and the constant joys and challenges that flow from Katie, Rachel, and Nate.

Introduction

Public Culture and Public Authority

Perhaps the most pressing concern now facing the church in the United States and the Western world is to understand better the tensions Christians experience as we live and minister in the midst of a contrary and even antagonistic culture. All around us we see signs that whatever we used to know of a Christian culture is disappearing fast. As we enter the twenty-first century, many Christians sense that even greater antagonism may characterize our experience in the future. We need to know whether to approach this age with "Christian resignation," which waits for "the city that is to come" and makes only minimal demands on public life, or whether to "join others in the larger human quest for a healthy public space, in the hope that on that journey we too will experience those mysterious and surprising inklings of a larger kind of love that can take concrete shape—even in the here and now—in new forms of citizenship and community."[1] Perhaps this quest for a healthy public space can also take place within the church, as it can be both the crucible of responsible life in community and a body that serves to cultivate true civilization.[2]

Signs of the Times

For Christian leaders, knowing the demands and pressures experienced by those in their charge means finding ways to encourage and instruct them

9

even as the cost of discipleship grows greater. The Christian in the marketplace or the academy, the mall or the voting booth, sees daily evidence of the chasm between the values and beliefs that should characterize the lives of the children of God and those that seem to drive contemporary culture. All of us want to understand the times, as the early Christians were commanded to do by the Apostle Paul (Rom. 13:11). This is as much an imperative for those of us living within the global postmodern culture at the beginning of the twenty-first century as it was for the first-century Christians in the hostile Roman Empire.

On September 11, 2001, the United States suffered a serious terrorist attack upon New York City and Washington, D.C. Significant national and global symbols were destroyed or damaged, thousands of lives were lost, and national life was seriously disrupted. In the immediate aftermath, collective national unity was high, and in time-tested manner the American people as a whole rose in a great outpouring of patriotism and generosity towards victims of the attack. The voices of dissent, who called for understanding of the motives of the terrorists, or who—as a few conservative Christian leaders did—suggested that America got what it deserved because of its cultural decadence, seemed small and irrelevant and were quickly dismissed by most Americans. Generally, resolve to rally around national leaders, respond decisively against the perpetrators, and keep American economic and community life going was strong.

One of the premises of this book, expressed in its subtitle, is that we live in a divided or fragmented culture in the United States. Has the state of the culture, as measured in the long-term trends depicted in the survey data cited here been reversed? Has the crisis that I suggest in chapter 7 might be the only source of unity now come about? Will the symbolic declaration of "war" on terrorism emerge as a defining national purpose? Does the church now have a different responsibility than those suggested in this work? This war has, as of this writing, taken the form of "protecting our way of life," which may indicate that the general desire is not for change but continuity of what was before; yet this may not be possible. Understanding why the United States represents something evil, to be hated and opposed, is one of the tough questions Americans seem to be wrestling with as they face the reality of terrorist attack.

In the few weeks after the attacks, national legislation granted sweeping powers to the president to carry out military objectives. Discussion was heavy in editorial pages and broadcast media about loosening restrictions on investigation, giving more extensive powers to law enforcement officials that may raise civil liberties questions, and permitting "dirty" covert activities overseas. Yet Americans want their way of life not to be affected, and we also are exhorted to continue on with work and life, not allowing the terrorists to terrorize us. There does not seem to be much impetus toward changes other than those necessary to improve security.

If what is shown in this book truly expresses deeply seated tendencies, then they will likely reemerge as Americans become accustomed to the new vulnerabilities and the crisis fears subside. On the other hand, as suggested above, the crisis may force a renewal of purpose, morality, and faith. Will the church be able to supply the moral foundation for such cultural renewal? The examination of the responsibilities of the church in this book may offer some ways in which that can occur.

In the immediate years before September 2001, Americans experienced a wide range of bewildering cultural signals:

- The dominant strains of popular culture, violent and appetitive, offered up in powerful visual images that seem to violate the Christian sense of reflective peace, human dignity, and control over the life of the eyes and the mind.

- The contemporary tendency not to reject religion as illogical or unscientific (as modernism did) but to regard it as therapeutic ("whatever works for you") with considerations of truth being irrelevant.

- The delinking of public competence from "private morality," which is now so common in our discussion of political leadership. In the late 1990s, Americans were presented with the spectacle of a disgraced president, who was exposed for immoral sexual acts in the White House and for lying publicly. He became only the second U.S. president to be impeached by Congress, yet he remained very popular and was not forced from office. His public defenses often cited a generally understood distinction between private and public morality.

- The unprecedented arguments consistently presented to the American courts that Americans have an inherent "right to die" at the times and by the means of their own choosing. Such cases could potentially give constitutional validation to acts previous generations would have considered evil—or at least beyond the sanction of law.

- The rash of cataclysmic "critical incidents" occurring in the United States in the late 1990s that aimed serious violence at major public institutions. Most notorious are the 1995 truck bombing of the Alfred P. Murrah Federal Building in Oklahoma City by an army veteran and member of a "citizen militia," and a rash of school shootings, including the violent and hate-filled attack on fellow students by two teenagers at Columbine High School in Colorado whose nihilistic messages shocked the nation.

- The emergence of popular culture figures as moral spokespersons—such as Dr. Laura Schlessinger, Oprah Winfrey, and Montel Williams—who seemingly fill the gaping abyss left by religious and political leaders, with television and radio programs that dispense moral judgments and attempt to guide American decision making.

- The popularity of professional philosophers who have set up philosophical "counseling" clinics to guide others and to help them find life's meaning. As reported by the *Washington Post* on October 31, 2000, many Americans are now turning to such clinics. "'The secularization of America has left many people in a moral vacuum,' said [Lou] Marinoff, who counsels clients by trying to find a philosopher or philosophic tradition that offers wisdom for their particular problem. 'If you don't belong to an organized religion, how do you develop morals? People need wisdom that can be distilled for use but not watered down to where it is useless. That is what we are here to provide.'"[3]

The national election of 2000 offered an unprecedented challenge to American political culture. As the closest election in American history, it pointed to an evenly divided electorate, with each presidential candidate receiving about 50 percent of the national vote and with the two houses of Congress becoming evenly divided. These branches of the federal government joined the already divided Supreme Court to suggest a true political-cultural split in the United States as a whole. A widely circulated electoral map depicting all the counties in the United States showed the vote concentrations for Democrat Al Gore to be in coastal and midwestern urban areas, with the vast majority of counties (mostly suburban or rural) being won by Republican George W. Bush. Survey analyses of the electorate showed cleavages of voter support largely along racial and moral-cultural lines, suggesting that no widely held political consensus could be found in America. "The only consensus in these results is that there is no consensus. America is of two minds, profoundly divided over the culture, the Clinton legacy, the scope of government, and what it wants Washington to accomplish. Those two minds have now each selected half a government. Reversing Deng Xiaoping's famous formula for China and Hong Kong, we now have two countries, one system."[4]

Even more troubling, as the election process stretched out over weeks, the uncertain results gave opportunity for concerns about system crisis, the stealing of democracy, and declarations that the presidential winner would not be legitimate because of doubts about his selection and the process used (including legal challenges and public-relations campaigns) to bring it about. "We may be watching the deconstruction of democracy in America," one commentator wrote.[5] "It is clearer now than ever before that what we have been witnessing in America these last two weeks is something only a smidgen less than an attempted legal coup," wrote another.[6] These dire warnings emerged even as established constitutional procedures functioned to bring about resolution of the disputed election without violence. Yet the election gave opportunity for commentators to expose troubling underlying trends and fears, pointing to deep fissures and uncertainties in the populace.

These fissures and uncertainties are expressions of the "public life" that defines and directs the way we live together in the United States in the new century. These aspect are not only political or legal but appear in the multitude of institutions and patterns of interaction that make up the communities and nation in which we live. To speak of public life is to speak summarily of the full range of social, aesthetic, economic, religious, governmental, legal, educational, recreational, and other sectors of the community in which we live.

There are many ways to try to understand the times and the expressions of public life. Intuition and common sense might give us hunches or partially conscious reactions to experiences; this level of understanding is vital, as it forms the basis for our evaluations and responses. Such thinking is God-given and worthy of cultivation.[7] What we learned from our parents or communities also gives us means to evaluate what we hear and see. The insights of thinkers, writers, and preachers help structure our thinking and our judgments. Our reflections, prayers, and observations also contribute as we build patterns of understanding and response. None of these tools are necessarily correct and complete, but they help form the manner in which we understand the times.

Understanding the Times Systematically

Another tool of understanding is the systematic measuring of certain observable phenomena. We know from experience that the shape of the society in which we live, even its hostility to Christian norms, is not a series of random occurrences but develops in patterns of practice and habits of mind. These patterns can be observed, described, and even categorized in ways that summarize them and make them accessible to us. Summation is a major component of the work of science, both natural and social. Such summation can seem to limit and even suffocate the real effect of experience, but it helps us to name and place what we experience and to compare it to other experiences. To interpret our experiences and to construct categories of interpretation in order to understand our world is a very human endeavor that we employ in all aspects of life. We do this in relationships, in work, in worship, even in efforts to understand ourselves.

For example, a collection of consistently expressed beliefs about political issues and structures we label ideology. We categorize musical expressions that have similar traits and name them jazz, hip-hop, baroque, and so on. In the same way, we can categorize and name certain patterns in the broad category of culture so we can talk and think about shared experiences in a commonly understood way.

Missionaries have long understood that commonly held ideas can make a group of people more or less open to believing and embracing the gospel— from matters as simple as whether they know what a lamb is, to the degree that strong ties of community, authority, or deeply seated traditions might inhibit an individual from making a personal decision for Christ. Turning the missionary challenge on the West, Bishop Lesslie Newbigin has written that contemporary Westerners have lost much of their ability to comprehend the gospel, since concepts such as moral responsibility, personhood, and natural order have been leached out of human consciousness by modern thought and life.[8] Long-term common practice reinforces, rewards, and sustains these cultural patterns. They are passed on to children and perpetuated over time.

Sources of Cultural Analysis

There are many sources of insight available to thinking Christians that can inform cultural and political analysis. All of these sources have biases, emphases, orientations, and histories that must be considered as we employ them. Yet, in the grace of God, they are among the many intellectual tools available for the comprehensive discipleship of the church in the new millennium. Three of these tools are significant for our study.

1. *History.* It has long been the proclivity of human beings to record their actions and to try to make sense of their collective behavior. Further, analysis and even repetition of these patterns through historical study have also been important aspects of maintaining the coherence and identity of any nation or society. It is possible for us to judge the current day by the lessons, insights, and answers of the past—to see the effects of chosen actions and to learn from them.

2. *The commentary of the wise.* Explanation and analysis are God's gifts to some who are set aside to serve church and culture through their writing and teaching. The Christian tradition has evinced this blessing from the beginning, and the church has preserved much of its received wisdom. Christian thinkers, from Irenaeus and Augustine in the early centuries to the great twentieth-century masters such as G. K. Chesterton, C. S. Lewis, Christopher Dawson, and many still living, have worked heartily to equip the church to face the challenges of its surrounding culture.

3. *Survey data.* Many surveys have charted the values, attitudes, and trends of American public culture through polling and other means of testing public opinion. These surveys measure current attitudes and behavior and provide either current snapshots or long-term trends. A survey is, of course, a limited instrument. It relies on self-reporting and assumes a level of truthfulness in respondents that may or may not be justifiable. Surveys can easily result in contradictory findings, since respondents can misrepresent themselves or report attitudes and behaviors that do not appear when measured in other ways. A survey cannot explore in depth what is in the mind of each participant, but it can look for indicators of patterns.

Many surveys provide an important set of measurements to accompany reflective works, and these results are considered in this book. They show, for example, the persistence of a high level of public dissatisfaction with the actions of governing officials alongside a high level of expectation that the federal government should be able to solve public problems. This sheds some light on the seemingly contradictory election results that put activist presidents in office along with antigovernment Congresses. If surveys do not explain why this occurs, they do highlight some of the thought processes that inform voting (or nonvoting) in the United States and indicate what the most influential forces and patterns at work in public life might be. Many surveys portray a fragmented, doubtful, and potentially revolutionary public mood, which raises questions about the viability of public support for the American experiment in democracy as it is being practiced today. Constant shifts in policy and contradictory election results may make a great deal of sense in such an environment.

Christians and the Formation of Authoritative Public Philosophy

Along with getting a clear understanding of the culture in which we live, a second set of questions face the church: Is it necessary for American society to have a common public ethic—a widely held public philosophy and sense of the common good—in order to sustain civil public life? And what responsibilities do Christians have to contribute to right public order in the cultivation of such a defining philosophy? Theologian Oliver O'Donovan, in his extensive 1996 work on political theology, *The Desire of Nations,* holds that a society obtains political identity and becomes a community through political acts—acknowledging legitimate authority and submitting to it.[9] According to O'Donovan, this demand for "authoritative formation" conforms to the biblical pattern—such as that seen in the covenants of ancient Israel—of the necessary establishment of public authority, and the recognition of its providential origin, as the constitutive act of society. If this is the case, then a society needs some central authoritative ideas that conform to God's designs for mankind in order to hold together. Further, a society that loses confidence in and turns away from established authority can expect serious difficulties and even breakdown.

Public surveys allow us to explore the extent to which such a common public philosophy is evident in the United States and whether it effectively relates people to authority and guides public life. If the United States is in a period of delegitimization—of declining authority and chaotic public identity, as many commentators hold—then the storm warnings identified in survey data may prove accurate. Christians must assess their role in forming, or restoring, an appropriate vision of public life, including the relationship between authority and society. We must also assess our role in sustaining legitimate social order and in dealing with the challenges to that order that prevail in American society as we enter the twenty-first century.

The goal of this book is to explore the insights of recent research on the public role of American Christianity and to signal the church regarding the state of the public culture in which it resides. The book is intended more for Christian leaders and informed laity who are guiding the public life of the church than for scholars of public policy and culture. But I trust the latter group also will find the analysis useful. I emphasize certain indicators emerging from analysis of survey data that either mesh with or challenge the insights of leading thinkers about the state of public life. These survey results, to use a meteorological analogy, call for a storm watch but not a storm warning, not immediate alarms but definitely a strong signal about the conditions that may be developing over the horizon. By giving a clear picture of the fragmentation and disorientation found in the United States—which we experience in daily life and sense all around us—this research suggests that chaotic times are ahead without predicting exactly what those times might be like. This book does not presume to prescribe a course of action for the church, nor does it seek to articulate an authoritative and persuasive public philosophy for the next century. This book actually expresses some uncertainty about such endeavors, but it provides some resources for those endeavors and indicates some aspects of the context in which that work must be undertaken.

Chapter 1 takes up the definition of terms and the structure of categories within which to analyze public life—these categories being culture, philosophy, and theology as they take broad public and more specifically political forms. Chapter 2 considers the historical context of Christian approaches to American culture, primarily the categories of understanding that shaped Christian public life for centuries in the West. The legacy of the church, it turns out, both guides and confuses the church in public life, as Christians tend to make use of comprehensive language from other eras in currently fragmented circumstances. Chapters 3 and 4 examine in depth some measures of current political culture from survey data and public commentary as they bear on the overall shape of public life—in particular, to discern whether any common authoritative philosophy or moral framework can be discerned at work in the United States. Chapter 5 marks the turn in the attention of this book to a more specific focus on the Christian commu-

nity and its current efforts at engagement with public life. In this chapter
I offer an overview of some of the themes to be found in current Christian
political thinking and relate them to various analyses of public compre-
hension of political ideas. Chapter 6 explores some of the effects of measured public attitudes on the church and its public witness, and Chapter 7
indicates some of the major challenges for the church and for public life in
the next century, as the church faces its public responsibilities in the new
world being shaped by multiple forces and movements.

Part I

Public Life
and Political Culture

For the day of the LORD is near upon all the nations. As you have done, it shall be done to you, your deeds shall return on your own head. For as you have drunk upon my holy mountain, all the nations round about shall drink; they shall drink, and stagger, and shall be as though they had not been.

Obadiah 15–16

There is no authority except from God, and those that exist have been instituted by God. Therefore he who resists the authorities resists what God has appointed, and those who resist will incur judgment.

Romans 13:1–2

1

Christian Resources
for Public Life
in the Twenty-First Century

The church faces an array of challenges—intellectual, moral, institutional, social, political, economic—as it approaches the new century. While many of these challenges are posed from within—such as questions about biblical authority, the role of women, new moral dilemmas, organizational unity, and interdenominational relations—many challenges come from the public context in which the church is set at the beginning of the twenty-first century. The church has a rich history of reflection and action regarding public life, much of which has been prompted by the need to sort out conflicting obligations between the city of God and the city of humanity, and some of which has been prompted by experiences of hostility, opposition, and persecution. The church carries on its temporal journey with the firm hope that comes both from its continuation through the rise and fall of cultures and empires and from the promises of the ultimate triumph of Christ and his kingdom. Yet the American church also carries into the new century the immediate legacy of recent history, which was, if Max Stackhouse is correct, "a time of vague, free-floating 'spirituality,' of little importance

21

for the great issues. Modern churches lacked social significance because, contrary to what had been the case in all the preceding ages, they lacked a high view of the Church." The twentieth-century churches in the West contrast with their ancestors, who knew that "ecclesiology is, indeed, essential to Christian social philosophy, since the Church is the place where persons are formed theologically and ethically to live responsibly in the wider society."[1] It has also been the understanding of Christians in many times and places that the church is a public body that both shapes and serves the building of civilization, and that there is no conflict between spiritual life and public life, as all are to be brought under the will and rule of God in the life of the Christian.

Resources for Facing the Challenges of Public Life

Three levels of analysis, or categories in which to place our observations of and responses to public life, will help to guide the church's responses to and activities in the public realm. These categories are a means of interpreting public life and acting accordingly. At the level of *culture analysis* we describe, categorize, and respond to the overall patterns of behavior and attitude that can be discerned in public life. At the level of *philosophy* we articulate systematized beliefs about the nature and structure of public and political life. And at the level of *theology* we explore the connection between the essentials of faith and public and political life. Each of these levels can be considered in both broad public and more particular political dimensions. And each level has been used by the church throughout its history to discern the times.

For many Christians, the ideal relationship of these resources would be to start with authoritative theology (the queen of the sciences), allow that discipline to shape philosophy, and use these together to guide patterns of involvement in public life. They want to follow the dictum that Oliver O'Donovan asserts as the need to "rediscover politics not as a self-enclosed field of human endeavor but as the theatre of the divine self-disclosure; to rediscover God as the one who rules."[2] We know that our convictions about the ultimate sovereignty of God and his historical purposes transcend all the temporal practices or cyclical patterns of human history. We want to know how these beliefs can structure our life on earth for the glory of God.

Further, we want our public judgments and challenges to be based on God's demands for human society, to the extent that we can know them.

Yet the reality is that understanding rarely flows in one direction and rarely starts with clear guidelines that lead to obvious practical implications. The cultural, philosophical, and theological levels are not wholly discrete and independent but are contiguous and interactive. Each informs the other. In public life, the truest picture is one of complex, multiple interactions between cultural experiences and systematic thinking. Many thinkers now stress the beliefs of a very influential school of analysis: that historical and immediate experience ought to have precedence and that reflection on experience should govern theological and theoretical pronouncement about the nature of public life. But even those who give precedence to established doctrine for authoritative guidance must also discover the practical meanings of these teachings through experience. Extreme examples help illustrate this: How do the few committed monarchists (who believe monarchy is God's pattern of governance) or the theonomists (who want to establish the full Old Testament law as the law of the land) realize their commitments and deal with the gap between these convictions and the current forms of law and governance? But more to the point for most Christians, if we believe government and other public institutions have some measure of responsibility to divine moral order and revealed truth, in what ways should this responsibility be expressed? And how do we evaluate the ways in which this responsibility is or is not being realized? What peace do we make with the practical limitations on the full realization of the glory of God that we experience every day in public life?

Public and Political: Defining Terms

The term *public,* now used so widely to refer to the arena with which this book is concerned, generally or simplistically refers to all that occurs outside of the household. But substantively, it incorporates what was in other times more commonly understood as "civic" or "community" life, or in classical times as "politics." The *Oxford English Dictionary* defines one sense of public as, "Of or pertaining to the people as a whole; that belongs to, affects, or concerns the community or nation; common, national, popular." For Aristotle, *politics* was the science of coordinating and making healthy all of life in the *polis,* or the whole community. The contemporary approach tends to differentiate society into economic, social, governmental, and other sectors, so now the broader term *public life* covers the same ground as "politics" once did. The concept of public life is not only *political,* in the modern understanding of that term as it refers to governmental and legal institutions; it points to the whole range of economic, political, social, and moral-cultural patterns and institutions that make up a community or a nation. It refers to the ways in which we live together corporately. The Latin origin of the term *republic* (*res publica,* or matters of the populace) helps clarify this usage. Another translation of this term, the English word *commonwealth,* points to the interweaving of what works together for our good, for the common well-being of all and for the community as a whole, if these institutions and patterns are formed and directed accordingly.

The church is included in this definition as a public institution, an entity in which people hold things in common and work toward common ends. It is a public space where things of public significance occur, in this understanding, and is a sector of a larger public life. It is divinely appointed (as are also, some would argue, government, family, and economic arrangements, and all other structures of existence) and is primarily responsible for ordering the right worship of God and the promulgation of divine revelation about salvation and the truth of the Trinity. The church is not merely an association of individuals each pursuing the fruits of personal salvation. It is the public representative of Christ, who is King of all the earth, the visible expression of his lordship and redemption.

Confusion about the church as a public institution can easily follow if this concept is translated into the church becoming an organized political power, an economic association providing jobs, goods, and services, or a health and welfare organization. Rather, worship and proclamation and commissioning are public goods that are the province of the church. This can be very difficult to grasp, perhaps especially for individualistic Westerners in the current age, who have learned to place worship, morality, revelation, and "personal growth" in the bin labeled "private" or "personal." Under these assumptions, to realize the need for a "public church" is to call for a political church that supports candidates, advances policy positions, organizes voters, and sponsors protests. Under a different understanding, a "public church" orders life in a certain way, primarily because it is the will of God and true to created human nature but also because doing so serves the larger common life of all.

The church, then, also serves as a public space in which men and women learn civility and are formed in the virtues that serve in the other arenas of public life. If one's life is rightly ordered at the core that the church shapes, the potential for rightly ordering the rest of life, public and private, is advanced. But the public service of the church is not only in training individuals; it is also in serving its purposes for the entirety of public life. For public life is not just the sum total of individual lives; it is the pattern of community responsibility and commonweal that constitute human existence, according to the creational purposes of the Creator.

Public Culture and Political Culture

The broad patterns of corporate behavior and belief that are labeled "culture" indicate a range of phenomena that summarize the characteristics of a group, community, or nation. These patterns encompass matters of belief, thought, and accepted common practices. They include but are not limited to artistic and literary expressions. The broad term *culture* summarizes "areas of human endeavor where symbols are created and adapted to human needs. . . . Culture orders our experience, makes sense of our lives, gives us meaning."[3] For Roger Lundin, "culture designates that complex, interlocking network of symbols, practices, and beliefs at the heart of a society's life."[4]

It almost goes without saying that American Christians have fully incorporated the term *culture* into their vocabulary. It is now typical to hear laments not only about legislation or public policy but also about cultural decline or patterns of immorality. Christian thinkers have referred to a "post-Christian culture" that lacks the moral authority and normative standards of other eras. John Paul II laments a growing "culture of death" in the West that presents major challenges to a life-affirming church.[5]

These cultural patterns have both public and private dimensions. *Public culture* refers not merely to public events or actions beyond the bounds of the home; it indicates patterns of belief, practice, and responsibility found in public life. It indicates which institutions (schools, churches, organizations, agencies) citizens are related to and hold responsible for aspects of community and national life. Public culture also has moral dimensions, for example, guiding acceptable and unacceptable public behavior. What is acceptable to talk about or to do in parks, in restaurants, at parties, on television? (Sex? Death? Medical matters? Politics? Religion? Personal wealth?) It indicates expectations for individuals as they participate in life beyond their private circles: for example, should everyone serve his or her country for a few years even if there is no draft or public service law? Public culture provides normative categories for life, such as whether group members are considered equal or subject to a hierarchical structure, what degrees of freedom are allowed or conformity is expected, and what are the roles played by various participants. Primarily, public culture sets out expectations by which public life is evaluated and guided and determines the meaningful truths by which it is shaped and structured.

John Paul II stipulates that

> it is not possible to understand man on the basis of economics alone, nor to define him simply on the basis of class membership. Man is understood in a more complete way when he is situated within the sphere of culture through his language, history, and the position he takes towards the fundamental events of life, such as birth, love, work and death. At the heart of every culture lies the attitude man takes to the greatest mystery: the mystery of God. Different cultures are basically different ways of facing the question of the meaning of personal existence.[6]

Political culture is a very large aspect of, though not the entirety of, public culture. Political culture indicates the beliefs, attitudes, and practices relating to the specifically political realm—the realm of law, defense, public order, and the authoritative coordination of public life. The field of political culture explores the underlying currents that are manifested in specific political behaviors and beliefs. These include not only regional and demographic characteristics but also the experiences and beliefs that may determine voting and participation patterns. Are leaders to be trusted or not? Are people in a given area inclined toward civic life, or do they leave public affairs to a few and focus on private interests? Is the government expected to solve major life problems or merely to keep minimal order? Can people be trusted to do right if left to their own decisions, or must they be forced to behave in ways not harmful to others? Is it possible for right and wrong to be known clearly enough that the law can be unambiguous about morally questionable acts such as drug use, abortion, and assisted death of the terminally ill?

Thus, to return to the weather analogy, it can be said that while following politics—in the sense of debating public policy, following elections, and so on—is like following the daily weather forecast, looking at political culture is like studying climactic conditions and other stable determinants of local weather. The politics of a society, like the weather, may change rapidly; but the normative context of political culture, like the climate, will change only very slowly. Changes in political culture have tremendous consequences.[7]

Numerous surveys and studies have explored political culture to provide a portrait of the state of political life in the United States today. Such studies measure the level of interest and participation in politics as well as explore concerns about the pressing issues of current political activity (balancing the budget, tax cuts, term limits, prayer in schools, defense spending, and so on). Other questions focus on the level of confidence in the government and its officials and the level of commitment to the historical values of the American republic. The results of these studies can be important resources for examining the culture in which public responsibility is to be undertaken in the twenty-first century.

The general picture the surveys provide is of an American political culture that now is fragmented, contradictory, and turbulent. While political institutions, parties, and procedures seem to be stable, the ground underneath them is starting to tremble. Americans express high levels of commitment to traditional public ideals, civic life, and civility in their public dealings, yet their level of trust and confidence in their leaders is generally down, and belief that the United States is in decline is very high, even in a period of prosperity and peace. The sources of these beliefs are harder to discern. (Do they result from years of assaults on the American way of life by intellectuals? From cynical media coverage? From years of experience of untrustworthy leadership? From a more general decline in trust of institutions? From economic or social shifts?) But the patterns of disturbance and disaffection emerging in political culture are clear. Moreover, these perspectives are very strong among Americans with deep religious commitments. They are strong also among Americans of middle income, professionals and workers, and white Americans—those who have been the traditional backbone of support for the experiment in ordered liberty. Why these patterns are appearing now is one of the primary ques-

tions that must be considered by anyone wanting to understand the times
and to act with responsibility in public life.

Public Philosophy and Political Philosophy

Public philosophy is a more systematic way of summarizing the content
of belief about public life. Whereas cultural analysis identifies operating
and effective ideas, philosophy charts out formal specifications or models
by which public and political life is shaped. Public philosophy is the way
in which we describe the public realm and formally assign roles and expectations for individuals and institutions. These are the ideas through which
citizens relate to and participate in society. They are also the ideas we use
to resist perceived aberrations of public roles and expectations. Public philosophy includes questions of public morality, equality, and how economic,
social, moral, and political institutions function and relate. These views can
be found in both informal and systematic forms. They are influenced and
shaped not only by experience but by basic moral and religious frameworks
as well.

For example, do we expect religious institutions, schools, families, or
some other institution to provide the basic moral framework for children? What rights do individuals have, and are these rights limited or
unlimited? Should family preservation and parental responsibilities count
more or less than economic growth and corporate success? Should religious institutions have special privileges and enjoy special protections?
Should any form of "expression" be permitted, even if it violates standards of decency? How should law, policy, or local custom regulate any
of these?

Is it possible to find a moral framework in America today? If so, what is
it? Further, does it really matter?

In *Moral Politics: What Conservatives Know That Liberals Don't,* George
Lakoff notes that these frameworks, or worldviews, can be attributed to
common sense, but that "common sense has a conceptual structure" that
is often unconsciously held.[8] Lakoff indicates that his work studying the
cognitive and linguistic patterns found in the American public demonstrates that certain categories of moral reasoning have strong resilience.
Commitment to responsibility, authority, community, reward and punish-

ment, and other "values" are deeply embedded in the beliefs of Americans. Thus, according to Lakoff's analysis, more conservative rhetoric and policies seem to have an advantage in American politics over liberal emphasis on freedom and nurture. A 1996 survey called *The State of Discussion* found that Americans overwhelmingly uphold the tenets of the "American creed" or the "American proposition" while being skeptical about the commitment of leaders and elites to fulfill those values may be similar to the finding put forth by Lakoff. The concrete beliefs and actions held by most Americans point to their underlying commitments. However, in terms that other analysts hold forth—that a public philosophy needs to be articulated, robust, and clear—these analyses indicate at best a thin consensus that may not be deeply embedded.

Political philosophy refers to specific categories related to the political realm: freedom, the role of law, the nature of political participation, the responsibilities of government, the definition of rights, and many other issues related to the behavior of government and the behavior of individuals and groups of citizens. The articulation of a coherent and viable political philosophy has been the goal of contending thinkers since the earliest human history. Ancient questions persist to this day, even as circumstances have changed over the centuries: Who should participate in civic and political life? Anyone? Men only? Property owners? Native-born citizens only? Who should lead? Should all moral questions be a matter of law? How are authority and legitimacy recognized?

Political philosophy also clarifies a particular vision of government, its structure as well as its roles in society and for individuals. Should government be a limited institution, concentrated on overt matters of public good and protection, or should it also be in the business of formulating individual character, creating families, guiding the training and development of children, guiding the economy, and promoting and perpetuating religion? What role does divine law play in civic institutions? In the United States, principles of federalism, separation of powers, election of representatives, civil rights, and limits on the power of national government are all central to the Constitution. These follow from a republican philosophy of the political community. Other ideological systems—such as socialism, conservatism, liberalism, Marxism—are built on political philosophy, because they start with assumptions about human beings, human community, and the forms of authority that should constitute political and social life.

Public and political philosophy is a professional pursuit for some, an avocation for many others. Whether it should be a concern of all citizens and whether it is necessary to orderly civic life is hotly debated today, especially since the American public seems not to hold in common any more than the most general public notions at this time in its history, and it holds those rather tentatively.

Definers and Critics of Public Philosophy: Sandel versus Rorty

The existence of and need for a comprehensive public philosophy has been a matter of extensive and vigorous discussion in the years surrounding the dawn of the twenty-first century. Harvard political theorist Michael Sandel, diagnosing the ills he perceives in American political life, asks:

> Why is American politics ill-equipped to allay the discontent that now engulfs it? The answer lies beyond the political arguments of our day, in the public philosophy that animates them. By public philosophy, I mean the political theory implicit in our practice, the assumptions about citizenship and freedom that inform our public life.[9]

Sandel asserts his belief that the currently prevailing liberal public philosophy—which emphasizes individual freedom without norms, celebrates economic success, and holds Americans to no common commitments— "cannot contain the moral energies of a vital democratic life. It creates a moral void that opens the way for narrow, intolerant moralisms. And it fails to cultivate the qualities of character that equip citizens to share in self-rule."[10] Sandel therefore calls for a "formative project," ill-defined in his 1996 book, but one nonetheless that seeks to "revitalize the civic strand of freedom"[11] and to "accord the political community a stake in the character of its citizens."[12] The shape of this philosophical project would account for the great diversity in the American population, address disparities of wealth and opportunity, and accommodate the increasing globalization of economics and some governmental functions, yet at the same time, it would acknowledge the significance of local communities. "Practicing self-government in small spheres, Tocqueville observed, impels citizenship to larger spheres of political activity as well."[13] Above all is the significance of the "narrative resources," so debased in the age of modern media saturation, that "tell the tales that order our lives."[14] We need to have a common story and common purposes as an American people. To achieve all this requires leadership, a cry for which ends Sandel's book.

By contrast, other contemporary thinkers consider the effort to expound a public philosophy a futile exercise, incomplete at best and oppressive at worst. These analysts advocate a much more open and pragmatic understanding of public life, leaving the problems of purpose and definition aside in favor of procedural and experiential solutions that are fluid, changing according to need and place. These thinkers are nonfoundational (or antifoundational) in clearly eschewing the formative project advocated by Michael Sandel and others. The very influential and oft-cited contemporary philosopher Richard Rorty calls for "us to dispense with the idea that scientific and political developments require 'philosophical foundations'— the idea that judgment must remain suspended on the legitimacy of cultural [practices] until we philosophers have pronounced them authentically rational."[15] For Rorty, this is not a problem, because it is possible to sustain core commitments—to liberty, civil rights, and just practices for example— because they work well and have survived the test of practice. As one commentator on Rorty explains:

> Rorty openly accepts the idea that these core commitments can never be buttressed by appeals to transcendental or ontological arguments but maintains that such philosophical reinforcements are not needed in the first place. All that is required to sustain a commitment to liberal democracy is a comparative historical narrative about the way in which its customs and institutions have, on the whole, made these societies less cruel and more free (i.e., tolerant . . .).[16]

Rorty exemplifies an approach that gives place to empirical experience, to the obligations and commitments made by humans as they go about their lives and attempt to live together in communities. Thus it is not necessary to appeal to universal theories of natural rights or any other abstract scheme of the good society. Rorty believes that guidance about public life comes from "our loyalty to other human beings clinging together against the dark, not our hope of getting things right." "The patterns of the past and the needs of the present" are sufficient guides, according to Rorty.[17] For analysts like Sandel, however, giving in to this way of thinking is the path to the decline and fall of America.

This brief review of current debate, sketched out in its simplest terms, barely touches on all the dimensions of these issues. But it mirrors debates also carried out in public discourse over specific policy approaches to education, medical care, welfare, even foreign affairs. Should education seek to develop virtue and character for citizenship, or should it concentrate on skills that make an individual economically productive and functional? Should human life be treated as sacrosanct, protected and nurtured at every stage, even if "defective," or is the value of human life measured primarily by practical contributions to the economy and society? Should the United States pursue only economic and security interests abroad, employing whatever means it takes, or should we advocate a vision of society, government, and human rights for other nations and carefully consider the morality of the available instruments of policy? Such issues are the policy windows into the deeper levels of public life that indicate whether we as a nation can sustain a common vision and be governed by it.

Christian Public and Political Philosophy

A similar discussion is found among Christian theologians and public thinkers, as well as in the church. Along with high levels of Christian activism, both "left" and "right," aimed at influencing public policy and public opinion, the volume of work attempting to sketch out a Christian approach to public life is enormous. Some contributions remain simple, as in the use of familiar biblical phrases to justify economic endeavors or particular public policies. But these endeavors are not limited to those who seek political power or results for particular organizations. Christians are also engaged in elaborate and systematic articulation of public philosophy, building on biblical and doctrinal principles to establish a comprehensive public framework.

The setting of these Christian projects has been the same as that experienced by all Americans: urbanization, the emergence of the United States as a world power, the Cold War and its demise, poverty, racial conflict, technological expansion, the information explosion, and the emergence of a globalized economic order. Perhaps of greatest significance has been the growing ethnic and moral pluralism within the United States, especially the need to understand the nature of public life in an age when the prior Christian consensus—such as it was—no longer holds. But for these projects, the uppermost concern has been to relate some understanding of Christian truth about the world and human existence to public life. Christians experience keenly the gap between God's standards for human life and the realities of a sinful, fallen world.

Christian public philosophy is inevitably grounded in some understanding of the implications of revealed truth and redemptive history for public life. Thus it is connected to theology, mediated traditionally through the field of ethics, or the consideration of the good in human life. For example, in *Centesimus Annus,* his 1991 encyclical on social and political life, John Paul II declared that

> from the Christian vision of the human person there necessarily follows a correct picture of society. According to . . . the whole social doctrine of the Church, the social nature of man is not completely fulfilled in the State, but is realized in various intermediary groups, beginning with the family and including economic, social, political and cultural groups which stem from human nature itself and have their own autonomy, always with a view to the common good.[18]

This succinct summary of a particular Christian public philosophy points to its theological foundations as the authoritative grounding of its assertions. The term *public theology* thus has been increasingly used to describe the search for these moorings. The issue is whether there is at base a moral order, a normative structure for human society, that has ultimate sources and even divine origins, and whether that order can be elaborated coherently and with actual effect on public life. Christian attempts at formative public philosophy interact with theological questions in all aspects of their analysis and prescription.

Public Theology and Political Theology

Within the realm of the church, where all human endeavors ultimately require grounding in the creating, redeeming, and sanctifying work of the Trinity, public life issues must be subject to theological inquiry and scrutiny. Such endeavors are ancient, with origins in the historical struggle of theocratic Israel, as narrated in the Old Testament, to develop faithful and coherent political and public life in the midst of hostile challenges from threatening and conquering civilizations. The birth of the church as the supranational and supracivilizational body of Christ on earth immediately raised questions for its leaders about Christian relationships to culture and government. The apostles Paul, John, and Peter wrote about these matters, as recorded in the New Testament, preparing the way for the systematic teachings of Augustine, Thomas Aquinas, Marsilius of Padua, Dante, Luther, Calvin, Hooker, and others, all the way to nineteenth- and twentieth-century "public theologians"—who run the range from the "social gospel," "Christian realism," liberation theology, Reformed, and Catholic varieties of institutionalism to advocates of prophetic alternative communities.

Public theology, therefore, seeks a basis found in Scripture and in the tradition of the church to validate, examine, and offer a critique of public life. This endeavor is also referred to as "social theology" (John Milbank), "social teaching" (Ernst Troeltsch), and various other terms. The major question propelling this effort has been to determine what role the church should play in the broader culture. Should it limit itself to Word, sacrament, and other "religious" activities, or should it also play a role in economics, education, health issues, and the military? In Ernst Troeltsch's classic formulation, should the church be sect, a self-contained spiritual body, or *ecclesia* (church), a public institution that interacts with and affects civilization?[19]

Further, public theology seeks to understand in fully biblical and systematic terms the meaning of public life, the role of its various expressions and institutions, and the validity of these expressions and institutions. What is the nature of earthly authority in light of revelation? For example, does the family have a special place in creation and redemption, therefore demanding special treatment and cultivation by the public sphere? What about property? Is private property a right that can gain theological sanction? Should property be held in common? Should economic activity pass a common-good test or conform to biblical standards? Does the state have any recognized role in redemptive history? The search for a common public philosophy has become a crucial undertaking for Christians seeking to evaluate the degree to which public life conforms to God's designs for human society.

Public theology, then, also addresses questions of public ethics. What can be considered right and wrong in public life, and on what basis? Christians, who understand that their first loyalty is to God and the kingdom, must ask: What does this primary loyalty mean for connections and potential commitments to their nation, communities, workplaces, and associations? What are Christians permitted to do in the various public spheres, such as participation in military forces, economic activity, and public entertainment? Do these spheres have validity in the intentions of God and in his historical redemptive work? Should news-making and policy-demanding concerns about poverty, military aggression, and political corruption be of any concern in light of eternity? Thus Christians will have special interest in learning whether common norms can be found in the American public that can guide public life.

The opposition of the public realm to the purposes and will of God, therefore, is also of concern in public theology. If the public realm is in some measure (or in its entirety) a realm of sin and rebellion, should not Christians be involved in opposition and exposure, perhaps even in destruction of public institutions? Do we stand, with Christ, above, against, or within culture (as in the classic formulation of H. Richard Niebuhr)? Where does the risen and ascended Christ stand in regard to existing culture? Christians have long recognized that these are matters neither for neglect nor to be left entirely to pragmatic negotiation; rather, they are matters that require authoritative direction from the expressed will of God. In the latter half of the twentieth century, to point to the most prominent examples, the experience of Christians under the Nazi regime in Germany and under the communist regimes in Europe and Asia informed the entire church about public responsibility, giving it heroes such as Dietrich Bonhoeffer and Jerzy Popielusckio and a record of reflection and action for life in the midst of hostility and oppression. This history has also demonstrated the effects of neglect of or accommodation to the course of secular public culture.

Political theology seeks specific understanding about the nature of government and community authority. What is God's intention for the political realm? Is there a clear connection between the historical redemptive work of God and the political institutions that have the responsibility of order and protection in earthly life? What is the meaning in any particular age of the apostolic injunctions, particularly Romans 13:1–7 and 1 Peter 2:13–17, to honor and uphold the reigning political order? What does it actually mean that rulers are "God's servant for your good" (Rom. 13:4) and that Christians should "be subject to the governing authorities" (Rom. 13:1)? How does this square with biblical depictions, such as found in the prophets and Revelation, of hostile and anti-Christian regimes that will fall in ultimate judgment?

Recent scholarly work indicates the continuing significance of these questions. In *The Desire of Nations,* Oliver O'Donovan begins his analysis with the proclamation found throughout the Scriptures—and made distinctly by Jesus—of the supremacy of the kingdom of God. He asks, "Is it meant to be the start of a new mode of political thinking? Or, is it, on the contrary, a stratagem for overwhelming politics with religion . . . ? When we call God 'King of kings and Lord of lords and only ruler of princes,' does that place the public business of our human communities upon a surer foundation? Or does it cancel it out . . . allowing us to conceive a God above and beyond politics?"[20]

O'Donovan goes on to argue for the relationship between political thinking and the understanding of religious truth, noting that "political theology is generally given to proposals . . . which draw out an earthly political discourse from the political language of religious discourse." He also presents a description of the results of political theology:

> Political theology . . . does not suppose a literal synonymity between the political vocabulary of salvation and the secular use of the same political terms. It postulates an analogy . . . between the acts of God and human acts, both of them taking place within the one public history which is the theatre of God's saving purposes and mankind's social undertakings.[21]

In other words, from an examination of the proclamation and historical unfolding of the kingdom of God and God's redemptive activity, one can draw principles and norms for earthly public and political life. Many thinkers have set themselves to this task.

John Milbank, in *Theology and Social Theory*, argues similarly that while much of theology since the Reformation, especially modernist and liberal theology, has been complicit in establishing the "autonomy of politics" (the separation of public life from theology), the work of political theology in the postmodern period is to restore "the possibility of theology as a metadiscourse." In other words,

> Theology has frequently sought to borrow from elsewhere a fundamental account of society or history, and then to see what theological insights will cohere with it. But it has been shown that no such fundamental account, in the sense of something neutral, rational and universal, is really available. It is theology itself that will have to provide its own account of the final causes at work in human history, on the basis of its own particular, and historically specific faith.[22]

But Milbank has little expectation of deriving a "deduction of Christian social teaching from Christian doctrine." He does not extract political principles from the doctrines of the kingdom as O'Donovan does. Rather, his public theology derives from "a distinguishable Christian mode of action, a definite practice."[23] This theology examines the characteristic modes of the church—as a reconciled community, its acceptance of differences rooted in creation, its demonstrations of peace—thereby standing in critique of secular society and modeling a different way. It will be the way the church acts, rather than its pronouncements, that will help shape public life. This claim will be explored further in this book.

For many Christians, especially evangelicals, perspective on public life turns on traditional theological questions, such as the meaning of creation, the effect of the fall, eschatology, and ecclesiology. If the end times and the coming of the kingdom will bring total destruction and judgment and a replacement of all that exists with a wholly new order, then political responsibility and reform in this world have hardly any importance other than survival. If, however, the coming kingdom is a restoration of the intended purposes of creation, a fulfillment of all that has been obscured by sin, then faithfulness in all realms of culture is called for.[24] Some Christians, such as those who espouse transformational or liberationist forms of theology, argue that the coming kingdom requires radical changes in earthly structures in order that they become more righteous and just. Similar questions are raised by the competing doctrines of the church. Does the church serve the purposes of the kingdom by looking forward to and anticipating another realm, or does it also have culture-building responsibilities now? Or are these possibly compatible, rather than contradictory, ends?

Some would argue that there is little or nothing in the Bible or in theology to give any clear practical guidance to public affairs. However, those who embark on the project of understanding the fuller prospects of creation and redemption have other convictions. Augustine, in *The City of God*, speaks for the conviction that the Holy Trinity is not detached from, but engaged in, public life:

> Therefore God supreme and true, with His Word and His Spirit (which three are one), one God omnipotent, creator and maker of every soul and of every body . . . from whom is everything which has an existence in nature, of whatever kind it be, and of whatever value . . . that God can never be believed to

have left the kingdoms of men, their dominations and servitudes, outside of the laws of His providence.[25]

These are matters that require extensive consideration, matters that have been dealt with for centuries; yet they form the context of the daily life and historical witness of the church. It is necessary for Christians to engage in these acts of understanding and interpretation as they face the public culture taking shape in this time of extensive change and challenge. Without this endeavor, the church easily falls prey to the spirit of the times and becomes its instrument. As the church considers its role in the formative project of American culture, its resources must be drawn from cultural analysis and interpretation as well as from Scripture and theological traditions.

Is it possible for the church to face and understand contemporary public culture, and then apply its theological and philosophical resources to shape and sustain a civil and moral public life in the new century? The church must attempt to interpret the cultural challenges it faces in ways that are true to its calling as the forerunner of the kingdom of God. The need to understand the challenges presented by the practices and beliefs in public culture, the need to clarify or comprehend a sense of what the public and political realms ought to be about, and the demand that these ideas and practices be founded on a sound sense of their relationship to the ultimate purposes of God are crucial aspects of the calling of the church to be faithful in its mission and witness as it enters the twenty-first century. Relating these aspects to each other is both difficult and necessary. But such an endeavor is an essential part of mission and discipleship as the church goes into all the world teaching men and women to obey all things that Christ has commanded.

2

The Historical Context

*The Inheritance
of the Christian Commonwealth
and American Pluralism*

And did those feet in ancient time
Walk upon England's mountains green?
And was the holy Lamb of God
On England's pleasant pastures seen?

And did the Countenance Divine
Shine forth upon our clouded hills?
And was Jerusalem builded here
Among these dark Satanic Mills?

Bring me my Bow of burning gold:
Bring me my Arrows of desire:
Bring me my Spear: O clouds unfold!
Bring me my Chariot of fire.

I will not cease from Mental Fight,
Nor shall my Sword sleep in my hand

Till we have built Jerusalem
In England's green and pleasant Land.

William Blake

Blake's evocative words convey, in the context of England, a legacy of social integration and comprehensiveness, a vision of a Christian commonwealth, a holy nation planted on earthly soil, a great dream of Jerusalem. In Blake's time, this vision had already been supplanted by secularism, the Enlightenment, and the industrial reorganization of society, prompting his crusading imagery of forming Jerusalem anew in his nation. Though Blake drew from many mythical sources and his own personal visions, and though his orthodoxy is not certain, he gives voice to a strong sentiment. He was followed a few years later by Alfred Lord Tennyson, whose *Idylls of the King* evoked the Arthurian legend of a Britain ruled by a Christian king leading the formation and extension of a holy society. The inherited legacy of the church in the West is one of an idealized Christian society, or Christian commonwealth, in which church and state and other institutions exist in harmony of purpose and commonality of order. But we now speak of the Christian commonwealth as the legacy of the church, rather than as its current cultural experience. As T. S. Eliot noted in the mid-twentieth century, all the "classical English treaties on Church and State . . . and indeed all up to the present time, assume the existence of a Christian Society"; but that no longer is the case.[1]

Blake's apocalyptic and poetic visions incorporated America into his concept of England, expressed as two great mountains separated by a flooded valley. This has historical resonance in the primary avenues by which the churches and political institutions of the United States came to be. The motivation of many early English settlers moving to America was to establish a "model of Christian charity" and to "be as a city on a hill, the eyes of all people . . . upon us," or to be a new Jerusalem. This is a defining myth of the founding period of the United States.[2] Further, many American churches retain in their liturgies and official declarations the assumptions developed in the context of a thoroughly Christian society. Calls for formation or reformation by many Christian activists are guided in great part by the vision that the church retains from its heritage of centrality to Western civilization and refers us back to that vision as we wrestle with the contemporary situation of the church.

Reformational Vision: The National Church in a Christian Society

> I am convinced that you cannot have a national Christian society, a religious-social community, a society with a political philosophy founded upon the Christian faith; if it is constituted as a congeries of private and independent sects. The national Faith must have an official recognition by the State, as well as an accepted status in the community and a basis of conviction in the heart of the individual.[3]

The vision expressed in Anglican polity—the tradition inherited by those jurisdictions descended from the established Reformation church of England—can serve as an example of the understanding of public life that was inherited by American churches. It is rich in complex historical and principled interconnection between ecclesiastical and civic order. Much of the history of the pre-Reformation church in England was marked by challenges over the nature and role of law and authority in the nation and the church. English churchmen since the earliest centuries of the Christian era sought to articulate in writing, counsel, and canon the roles and demands of these two ordained orders.

The settlements of the English Reformation and its aftermath married the church clearly to the parliamentary-monarchal order, attempting to bind the two estates under one national head and one national law; yet these settlements were continually subject to challenge and revision. Such uncertainty and challenge are a mainstay of the life of the church militant in yet-to-be-fulfilled history, as the church is given the knowledge of and is subject to supreme, divine authority while yet living in the world of delegated authorities and original sin. "From a theological perspective, it is arguable that all public disagreement is fundamentally about authority and law, divine and human, whatever may be the ostensible issues."[4] Who has authority for what, and under what conditions, are constant questions in the history of Christian culture. While the English Reformation attempted to "hold out an integration of faith and polity that does not admit of prophetic and eschatological criticism,"[5] tension and conflict between the two spheres helped to prod the search for other formulations, including the delineation of and limitation on the power of each. Yet there was never any sense that the two should be separated or that anything less than eternal principles were at stake in the formation of Reformation society.

Upon the independence of the United States from the United Kingdom, the framers of the American Anglican church translated the traditional church structure into a setting in which establishment was forbidden, but they conveyed to the new church the general legitimacy of the civic order, which had been embodied in the ancient relationship of the two estates bound under one earthly governor. The English canon lawyer Hubert Box sums up this prevailing view of legitimacy and shared responsibility, and the general Aristotelian conception that guided this understanding of creational orders:

> The Church is the only perfect supernatural society, and the State is the only perfect natural society. Man naturally tends to form society, and since no body of men could live together in peace unless they were subject to a supreme authority, God has given to the rulers of human society authority to look after the common weal. The State has a negative function in protecting those that make it up in the possession and exercise of their rights; and it has a positive function in promoting and furthering their welfare. But it cannot exercise these functions unless it has authority; and since they are demanded by a natural necessity of man, it follows that such authority comes from God.[6]

The significance of this understanding of divine order on earth cannot be underestimated. Governance of earthly society has divine origin and purpose, which is to be fulfilled in ways appropriate to its vocation. It thus is part of God's kingdom, of his will being done on earth as in heaven. Unlike the radical or Anabaptist Reformational perspectives, which tend to dismiss the significance of earthly kingdoms as corrupt or at best as a necessary evil, earthly order in this view has its proper calling and role for the fulfillment of human purposes. And unlike the earlier Roman Catholic beliefs that earthly governance should be subordinate to the universal church and its ruling papal structure, earthly society here is seen as perfect, in the sense that it has purposeful existence and an appropriate end and structure.

Yet the American church, in part under the influence of the Puritans and the colonial experience and its new principles, also declared a clear differentiation between the temporal and spiritual authorities.[7] They sought to prevent the "wicked confederacy between two systems of tyranny" that they perceived as characteristic of the English system, which "stipulated . . . that the temporal grandees should contribute everything in their power to maintain the ascendancy of the priesthood, and that the spiritual grandees in their turn should employ their ascendancy over the consciences of the people in impressing on their minds a blind, implicit obedience to civil magistracy."[8] Rather, "their greatest concern seems to have been to establish a government of the church more consistent with the Scriptures and a government of the state more agreeable to the dignity of human nature than any they had seen in Europe, and to transmit such a government down to their posterity with the means of securing and preserving it forever."[9]

The overall development of the magisterial Reformation tradition, especially as lived out in the American experience, can be traced from the Erastianism (a term indicating royal governance of church and state) elaborated by English luminaries such as John Wycliffe, Sir John Fortescue, Thomas Cranmer, Thomas Cromwell, and the Tudors and Stuarts, which bound church and state under one temporal head and gave them overlapping and interwoven responsibilities, to the "principled pluralism" expressed in the twentieth century by writers such as J. N. Figgis and Oliver O'Donovan, which sees church and state are separate but interwoven estates with designated spheres of responsibility that are yet founded upon common, universal divine order that they both serve. In this view, church and state serve to define and delimit the power and jurisdiction of the other, and the temporal head of one is not to head the other. Such is the perspective of the American expression of the Anglican tradition, as seen in its prayers and declarations.

Provisions in the Book of Common Prayer and the Articles of Religion

The Book of Common Prayer

The traditional *Book of Common Prayer* (BCP) served as the standard for regular worship and community in the Anglican churches and as the primary formulary for the church in its relation to civil authority and public life. Although there were many revisions made in the familiar 1979 American version and in the prayer books of other Anglican provinces, all previous versions—including the American versions through the 1928 edition—had retained the Reformational understanding of Thomas Cranmer's sixteenth-century formulations. Cranmer's original prayers are still to be found in the standard prayer book of the Church of England. In the prescribed orders for prayer, and even in the central eucharistic celebration, Anglican belief is proclaimed. The principle of *lex orandi, lex credendi* (the prayed law is the one believed), rather than doctrinal confession or catechism, serves as the primary means by which the church declares its principles of public order. In the "prayer for the whole state of Christ's church"[10] and in the supplemental prayers of the daily offices, Anglicans pray for limited yet effective civic rule and for the life, wisdom, and salvation of officeholders. These prayers seek to follow Paul's teaching in Romans 13:1–17 regarding the divine origin of civil authority, and its elaboration of specific duties of keeping public order, promulgating the law, and "serving the people for their own good."

In the prayers for the whole state, God is asked to order civil authority and "to direct and dispose the hearts of all Christian rulers that they may truly and impartially administer justice, the punishment of wickedness and vice, and the maintenance of true religion and virtue."

These are noble and high callings for civil authority, indicating that such authority is in the divine order of creation, that its role is that of servant to God and to citizens, and that law and justice are at the center of its purpose. The assumption of a Christian society is embedded in the prayer for "Christian rulers." Further, as dependent clauses are used to amplify the primary disposition (*that* they may truly administer . . . *to* the . . .), it is seen that among the first effects of the administration of justice are to be both the restraint of evil and the upholding of religion and public virtue. While there is little space here to exegete each of these phrases, it is clear that they call for a limited but purposeful government, one whose actions are informed by divine standards of right and wrong expressed as law. The instruction regarding "maintenance of true religion and virtue" at the least demands a government that does not inhibit the life of the church and the public proclamation of morality, and it opens the door for more direct governmental engagement in promoting public piety and character. This form for prayer is the same as that of the Church of England, where the state does have direct responsibility for the church. This prayerful statement of belief thus serves as proclamation and instruction to civil authorities of their purpose and calling and forms a viable constitutional core for the structure and limitation of public polity.

Beyond this central prayer, the daily prayers for officials ask God to remind them constantly of their true calling as servants of the common good and ties their activities to God's purposes in creation and redemption. For example:

> Almighty God, whose kingdom is everlasting and power infinite; Have mercy upon this whole land; and so rule the hearts of thy servants the President of the United States, the Governor of this State, and all others in authority, that they, knowing whose ministers they are, may above all things seek thy honor and glory; and that we and all the People, duly considering whose authority they bear, may faithfully and obediently honor them, according to thy blessed Word and ordinance; through Jesus Christ our Lord, who with thee and the Holy Ghost liveth and reigneth ever, one God, world without end. Amen.[11]

The Articles of Religion

The Articles of Religion constitute another formulary providing authoritative direction on some specific aspects of civil life and on the relationship of the church to civic order. The American Articles (as adopted in 1801) follow in order and direction the English Articles (of 1662, operative at the time of American independence), yet they offer a much more republican interpretation of the primary teachings found in the prayers.

Article 37 ("Of the Power of the Civil Magistrate") is the most direct address on these matters in the formularies. It pronounces the circumscribed power of the state and the extensive but limited obligations of citizenship. The use of the phrase "civil magistrate" defines the sphere being addressed and suggests the nature of the authority. *Magistrate* is an ancient term that conveys the idea of "delegated" or "granted" authority (rather than inherent sovereignty) and is primarily concerned with the administration of justice under the law. Thus the article is not about the "sovereign power" or the "supreme authority." The American article summarizes the more explicit teaching of the English article regarding the defined authority of the king (to whom is given the "chief government" in all estates, ecclesiastical and civil) in each realm. The American article extends the power of civil authority to "all things temporal" but gives no authority in "things purely spiritual." This also summarizes the *potestas ordinis* explication of the English article, that the civil magistrate does not have authority regarding Word and sacrament but has responsibility to provide order and protection to all estates, using the "civil sword" to restrain evildoers, to punish crimes, and to defend the nation.

The American article then makes a sweeping but clear and powerful statement regarding Christian citizenship: "[It is] the duty of all men who are professors of the Gospel, to pay respectful obedience to the Civil Authority, regularly and legitimately constituted." Thus the Anglican way is not one consigning the civil realm to the kingdom of darkness, from which separation is demanded. This echoes the English article that obligates Christians to recognize the legitimacy of the laws of the realm. It perhaps also incorporates the English provision for Christian participation in just wars as an aspect of "respectful obedience."

The American article, however, is very explicit in a matter that the English article assumes. The condition of obedience, that civil authority be "regularly and legitimately constituted," is a powerful phrase containing unspoken volumes. This provision, unlike the English article, grants to the Christian citizen and to the church the power of consent and the obligation to make judgments of legitimacy. Historically, this phrase validates the American founding experience and the constitutional doctrine that guides the American republic. It also implicitly anticipates situations in which authority may be irregular and illegitimate, either in its constitution or in its exercise. Thus civil authority is limited not only to the temporal realm but also to the rightly ordered exercise of law within the temporal arena. Protest, opposition, ordered efforts to change injustice, and even resistance in certain circumstances, are valid expressions of Christian citizenship under the terms of this article.

Articles 38 and 39 each address a specific concern, both of which had specific historical reference but point to persistent issues. The American articles follow very nearly the wording of the English. Article 38 permits the holding of private property, dismissing the Anabaptist (and by extension, other communist, socialist, and perhaps feudal) teachings about commonality of goods. The article (though in the negative) teaches that "riches and goods" in "right, title and possession" are not common, thus upholding responsible property ownership. The article demands responsible stewardship of property and condemns selfish hoarding through the insistence on liberal "almsgiving." This is the duty of "every man" rather than a collective responsibility. The protection of property right and title thus can be considered a legitimate temporal function of civil law. This would extend also to associational holdings, including that of the church, supporting the more explicit property protection provisions of the canons. "Everything created by God is good, and nothing is to be rejected if it is received with thanksgiving; for then it is consecrated by the word of God and prayer" (1 Tim. 4:4).

Article 39 permits the swearing of official and legitimate oaths "when a Magistrate requireth, in a cause of faith and charity, so it be done according to the Prophet's teaching, in justice, judgment and truth." These multiple conditions both prevent the "rash and vain swearing" condemned in Scripture that humans regularly indulge in and guide the situations in which oaths may be necessary and correct. These would include legitimate oaths of loyalty and fealty to "regularly and legitimately constituted" authority, such as upon taking office, and oaths to uphold the truth in legal proceedings. The sanction of oaths underscores both the support of legitimate authority as previously specified and the centrality of the law and just legal procedures. It is fitting that the final words of the Articles, "justice, judgment and truth," bind all Christian people, ruler and ruled, magistrate and citizen, to divine law and divine order, and to commitment to the truth in all things.

The Legacy of the Church of England and the Ancient Canons

Along with the *Book of Common Prayer* and the Articles of Religion, the English church also conveyed the regulations of the church recorded in the ancient canons (those drawn from the historic councils) and the then current canons of the English church to inform and guide the formation of the American church. The most notable contrast is that the American church chose not to codify directly the relationship of the civil magistrate to the church in canon law. They instead left it to the general guidelines of the *BCP*, the Articles of Religion, and the nonestablishment requirements of the federal Constitution. The operative 1603 English canons were explicit in both the submission of the church to the English king and the requirements of loyalty on the part of clergy and laity. Canon 1 required all clergy to keep, and to cause all others to keep, all laws and statutes "made for restoring to the Crown of this kingdom the ancient jurisdiction over the State Ecclesiastical" and through teaching, sermons, and other means to declare "that the King's power . . . is the highest power under God; to whom all men, as inhabitants, as born within the same, do by God's laws owe most loyalty and obedience, afore and above all other powers and potentates in the earth."[12]

The 1603 canons carried on the tradition of Christendom that the law and the legitimacy of the decisions of all authoritative bodies are embodied in the person of the prince, including the authority to call councils and validate ecclesiastical legislation. Further, the Reformation settlements, repudiating papal authority, placed the "chief government" in the king. The king is the highest representative of the law. Yet even these canons indicate an understanding of separate spheres, spiritual and temporal if you will, in that the submission of the church is to the person of the king, whose powers are circumscribed, and not to the state or the government. The canon presumes an integrated, coherent Christian commonwealth. John Henry Blunt's rather gentlemanly summary of the centuries of bloody conflict that led to this understanding elaborates these concepts:

> The idea of the Church being one body and the State another body is one of modern introduction. In former days the Commonwealth of England and the Church of England were considered as coterminous; those who were members of one also being members of the other. . . . But in modern phraseology the term "State" has come to represent not an "estate" of persons, but a concrete abstraction of the legislative and executive functions of the body politic. . . . The relations between "Church and State" are therefore the relations between all members of the Church of England . . . and the whole body politic of the kingdom. . . . The general principle of these relations is, that the Crown possesses a visitatorial and corrective jurisdiction in the Church of England, by right of which the sovereign is supreme governor over all persons and all causes ecclesiastical, as well as over all persons and in all causes temporal, within its dominions.[13]

Blunt then goes on to indicate that the Church of England was never officially "established" in the sense that the State chose one church to be the official religion. Rather, from the founding of the Church in Roman times, the gradual "Christianization" of the State by the Church "legalized its operations, and secured to it certain constitutional principles." Thus a system of privilege and restraint grew up; but the "establishment" of the Church has been effected in reality by its gradual assimilation with our national life, and not by Act of Parliament.[14]

The limitations on the power of the king as specified in the English Articles were in effect at the time of independence of the United States and the American church, and served as an elaboration of the first few of the 1603 canons regarding the "King's Majesty." These elaborations and the nascent understanding of separated spheres provided precedent and justification for the inauguration of an American church that suddenly found itself not tied to the necessity of royal supremacy or to any direct civil governance, in spite of having adhered to the laws of submission to the crown prior to 1785. Through its development of the concept of the civil magistrate, however, it did incorporate the legitimacy and divine vocation of civil society and of its directive agencies.

In both formulary and practice, however, the governance of the English church remains positively directed by parliamentary legislation and by state political processes even today, including the many appointments that remain the responsibility of the monarch, confusing the principled separation found in the formularies. This has to do with the development of constitutional law and political practice in England, as parliamentary power increased over the centuries since the time of James I, and with the maintenance of the tradition of monarchal governance. The English church has in many ways become more self-governing, such as through the creation of its General Synod, but that body is still subject to ultimate civil oversight and approval. English practice and polity at the time of the promulgation of the 1603 canons included the Reformation settlements, elaborated in the Restoration legislation, that regulated worship and polity by civil law and punished nonconformity. The canonical silence of the American church serves to underscore the distinctions between the two churches. However, the authority of the magistrate over "things temporal" in American Article 37 grants (unspecified) jurisdiction over many matters, and perhaps can be construed to include many matters not directly related to Word and sacrament. But American practice, as well as the canons directly governing the affairs of the church, transfer many of the temporal things of the church to the sole purview of the church itself, including the powers of appointment, election of bishops, and internal discipline.

The Legacy of the Magisterial Reformation

The full corpus of the formularies does provide in broad outline a concept of the role and function of civil government, which is primarily the promulgation and application of law and the provision for the public good and moral ordering of life. The formularies also assume the legitimacy of the civil order, its providential origins, and the obligations of citizenship. Civil government is to be legitimately ordered, or constitutional. Among the obligations of Christian citizenship, along with submission and consent, is the responsibility of regular prayer. The "prayed creed" of the *BCP* recognizes that through "common grace," providential order and sustenance are the active agents in civil order. Prayer is not only petition; it is an act of recognition and a submission to divine order. The Lord's Prayer is in many ways an "oath of fealty" to God's kingdom, as well as a plea for his continual governance on earth.

Canon law and the other Anglican formularies recognize that civic order, just as the ecclesiastical, is a legitimate and purposeful aspect of God's will and creation. Yet apart from a few explicit and established provisions, these formularies largely leave specific questions of citizenship to the exegesis of Scripture and the exercise of prudence. It would seem that the American formularies also incorporate (selectively) the more explicit instruction of English Article 37 for guidance in more general language—of course, eliminating the "chief power" of the king. That provision also separates and limits the spheres of authority and permits (not requires!) capital punishment and service in the military, indicating the obligations of citizenship to demand justice, protect life, and defend the nation. Yet citizenship remains largely an arena where custom, conscience, and prudence lead. Given the premise, as stated in English Article 37, that the only prerogative of the state is to "rule estates and degrees permitted by God," and given the general sense of the supremacy of the law over specific policies and the privileges of particular rulers, it is not impermissible to differ, protest, and even disobey when the state violates its bounds. This is clearly the case when the state attempts to prevent the church from its stated responsibilities. Yet it is also the duty of the church to recall for the state its own responsibilities and bounds, to pray for it, and to work within it for the common good.

The Puritan inheritance, also of central historical effect in the United States through the legacy of those who established the New England colonies, carries a similar understanding of civil order, with some pertinent differences that influenced the development of the American system. Calvin's *Institutes of the Christian Religion* laid the groundwork for this understanding, which was incorporated both in the formularies of Anglicanism and in those of the dissidents who broke from the established church in the seventeenth century. The final chapter of *Institutes* is devoted to the subject of civil government and plainly states that "the spiritual kingdom of Christ and civil government are things very widely separated."[15] Nonetheless, he then indicates that the "distinction does not go so far as to justify us in supposing that the whole scheme of civil government is a matter of pollution, with which Christian men have nothing to do."[16] Indeed, civil magistrates "have a commission from God, . . . they are invested with divine authority, and in fact represent the person of God, as whose substitutes they in a manner act."[17] The primary function of the magistrate is as "president and guardian of the laws," and the law is of divine origin.

Thus the Westminster Confession of Faith, developed by the Puritan and Presbyterian Assembly in 1646, during the dominance of the Long Parliament but before the execution of Charles I and the temporary abolition of the monarchy, follows closely the forms of the Thirty-nine Articles yet elaborates further on the distinct role of the "civil magistrate." This elaboration, undertaken during the early years of the American colonies, still gives a strong indication of the divine calling of the civil rule, yet it gives no possibility of subordination of church to state or vice versa. Further, following Calvin and the general understanding that there should be no separation of faith and public life, the king has responsibility for the protection and advance of true religion in a similar manner to that found in the Thirty-nine Articles. In chapter 23, "Of the Civil Magistrate," the Confession states:

I. God, the supreme Lord and King of all the world, has ordained civil magistrates, to be, under Him, over the people, for His own glory, and the public good: and, to this end, has armed them with the power of the sword, for the defence and encouragement of them that are good, and for the punishment of evildoers.

II. It is lawful for Christians to accept and execute the office of a magistrate, when called thereunto: in the managing whereof, as they ought especially to maintain piety, justice, and peace, according to the wholesome laws of each commonwealth; so, for that end, they may lawfully, now under the New Testament, wage war, upon just and necessary occasion.

III. Civil magistrates may not assume to themselves the administration of the Word and sacraments; or the power of the keys of the kingdom of heaven; yet he has authority, and it is his duty, to take order that unity and peace be preserved in the Church, that the truth of God be kept pure and entire, that all blasphemies and heresies be suppressed, all corruptions and abuses in worship and discipline prevented or reformed, and all the ordinances of God duly settled, administrated, and observed. For the better effecting whereof, he has power to call synods, to be present at them and to provide that whatsoever is transacted in them be according to the mind of God or, in the least, interfere in matters of faith. Yet, as nursing fathers, it is the duty of civil magistrates to protect the Church of our common Lord, without giving the preference to any denomination of Christians above the rest, in such a manner that all ecclesiastical persons whatever shall enjoy the full, free, and unquestioned liberty of discharging every part of their sacred functions, without violence or danger. And, as Jesus Christ has appointed a regular government and discipline in his Church, no law of any commonwealth should interfere with, let, or hinder, the due exercise thereof, among the voluntary members of any denomination of Christians, according to their own profession and belief. It is the duty of civil magistrates to protect the person and good name of all their people, in such an effectual manner as that no person be suffered, either upon pretense of religion or of infidelity, to offer any indignity, violence, abuse, or injury to any other person whatsoever: and to take order, that all religious and ecclesiastical assemblies be held without molestation or disturbance.

IV. It is the duty of people to pray for magistrates, to honour their persons, to pay them tribute or other dues, to obey their lawful commands, and to be subject to their authority, for conscience' sake. Infidelity, or difference in religion, does not make void the magistrates' just and legal authority, nor free the people from their due obedience to them: from which ecclesiastical persons are not exempted, much less has the Pope any power and jurisdiction over them in their dominions, or over any of their people; and, least of all, to deprive them of their dominions, or lives, if he shall judge them to be heretics, or upon any other pretence whatsoever.

The authoritative guidance, then, of the major traditions that shaped American colonial governance, and later cooperated in the formation of the United States as an independent nation, built on concepts of church, state, and culture that granted each of these realms the status of divine calling and understood that each had responsibility for the proper and effective realization of the callings of the others. This background of interwoven authority remains both the point of reference as well as the official doctrine of much of the church in America even at the turn of the new millennium.

Medieval and Catholic Vision: Universal Christian Society

The Christian commonwealth of the magisterial Reformation was an attempt to translate a Christian social and political vision into new concrete national structures. Strong states with new national identities, as they sought to be independent of universal and imperial claims of the Roman church and the vestiges of the Holy Roman Empire, inherited from the Middle Ages an understanding of integrated existence and singular authority that was to be expressed nationally.

T. S. Eliot sums up this medieval vision: "A Christian organization of society—which is not the same thing as a society consisting exclusively of devout Christians . . . would be a society in which the natural end of man—virtue and well-being in community—is acknowledged for all, and the supernatural end—beatitude—for those who have the eyes to see it."[18] Eliot wished to realize that vision in his day, the mid-twentieth century, and not to leave it to past ages. Yet for Eliot, and for many others who have charted these changes, the realization of that vision requires renewal, education, and restoration of a lost vision.

This vision is an understanding of life that does not easily separate temporal and spiritual, natural and supernatural. It understands all of life—

social, political, spiritual, and personal—as integrated under universal purpose. In commenting on the shaping influence that Augustine and Benedict had on Western life, James S. Taylor writes that this

> was no lark or quaint period of history but was the single, most transforming cultural force in the rebuilding of Western Europe [after the fall of Rome], informing in one way or another all those aspects of what is called "civilization" to such a degree that virtually every person of Christian medieval society, from popes and pirates and peasants, viewed the world as a vibrant arena of visible and invisible reality.[19]

In contrast, Taylor writes:

> Only after the Renaissance and Cartesian revolution in philosophy does a less intuitive, less integrated view of man emerge. By the twentieth century, the idea of objective reality—and man's various responses to it—has been eclipsed, for the most part, by subjectivism and a less certain, more lonely and mechanistic model of the human being and the universe.[20]

C. S. Lewis sums up the medieval worldview as "the medieval synthesis itself, the whole organization of their theology, science, and history into a single, complex, harmonious mental Model of the Universe . . . Its contents, however rich and various, are in harmony. . . . everything links up with everything else; at one, not in flat equality, but in a hierarchical ladder" of purpose and order.[21] Lewis goes on to show that this model was still at work in the poets, writers, theologians, and leaders of the sixteenth and seventeenth centuries, though their world was starting to move away from adherence to it.

The medieval model retained not only a powerful hold on those who formed the institutions that began the modern era and were carried to America but it also remains the background, the reference point, against which we identify the fragmented and ambivalent culture of the new millennium. Many have charted this journey, not only in intellectual history but also in social, political, and commercial life as well. The Canadian philosopher Charles Taylor, for example, observes in the emergence of the modern novel the collapse of the understanding of all of life as expressive of and saturated with divine purpose. Its form both expresses and reinforces the demise of the view of the world as the embodiment of archetypes, the world of the ontic logos. . . . The nature of a thing, I have argued, is now seen as within it in a new sense. We have to scrutinize the particular to arrive at the general. This was not just a principle of natural philosophers, but part of the way people came to understand their lives. Any other mode of narration now seems strange to us.[22]

The political and social integration and order of the medieval era is understood by many to have been imperfect, incomplete, often violent and inegalitarian. While there are those who idealize the medieval era, the nature of much analysis of this era is to characterize the form of its vision as it stands in contrast to later eras. Others would reject the medieval order, often under the label of "Constantinianism," in reference to the Roman emperor whose recognition of Christianity led to the social form that intimately linked church and state. Robert Wilken elaborates:

> The ritual pronouncement of anathemas against Constantinianism has become so commonplace that the historical Constantine (A.D. 288?–337) has slipped from our sight. Apparently it is not what Constantine himself wrought that is the object of obloquy, but the work of mischievous kings and perfidious bishops in the centuries after him. When theologians write essays with such titles as "Is Constantinianism the Most Basic Problem for Christian Social Ethics?", Constantine is not the sole villain. What provokes critics' ire is an ordering of Christian society that flourished in medieval and early modern Europe and still, it is claimed, impedes an authentic Christian witness.[23]

Wilken's challenges this perspective, represented by such thinkers as John Howard Yoder, Stanley Hauerwas, and Jürgen Moltmann,[24] with a historical and theological argument:

> There were, to be sure, unholy tradeoffs, and as Christian societies took form, kings and princes sought to manage the affairs of the Church and to use her spiritual authority to serve their ends. But even when the Church and the society were one and the king was considered head of the Christian people, the Church retained its distinctive identity. . . . The truth is that some form of Constantinianism is an inescapable consequence of the Church's success. Because Christians confess one God who is creator of everything that is, as

their numbers increase they will inevitably strive to transform all of life and society. The Church must say yea as well as nay to the world.[25]

The purpose of this study is not to evaluate the merits of the medieval or any other comprehensive vision but to demonstrate the degree to which that integrated vision informs the current attempts at Christian formation. It is a question worthy of investigation and argument, for example, whether the Crusades were driven more by the need to impose a universalist vision on all the world, or by impulses towards imperialism and economic dominance. The universal catholic vision of the Middle Ages shaped not only the development of national and colonial Christian societies in later periods but also the institutions that governed them. If such analysts as Eliot and Wilken are correct, a fully formed Christian philosophy will insist on expression in institutional arrangements and in policy, as has been seen historically and rhetorically. These arrangements may indeed be corrupted in ways that lead to persecution, inequality, or rigid conformity. But the diversity and fluidity of social arrangements throughout the Middle Ages suggest that it might be otherwise, as does the commitment to freedom and pluralism of many successors to the medieval vision.

At the center of the medieval vision, which carried into the social arrangements of the magisterial Reformation, is the understanding of law—especially the natural law—as God's order for all that lives. The primary responsibility of those granted power was to make known, to promulgate, and to execute law; thus the term *magistrate* is connected to the authoritative elaboration and application of the law. Many have noted that the influence of Augustine stands above all others in shaping the medieval concept of natural law, and through such dominant figures as Gratian, Thomas Aquinas, Alexander of Hales, and Hugh of St. Victor, it was conveyed to the Reformation and to us today.

> In the *De libero* we read that "The eternal law is the highest reason, which is always to be obeyed, through which the wicked deserve misery, and the good deserve the good life, through which the temporal law is rightly administered and rightly modified. . . ."
>
> Since all things are created by God and fall under the ambit of divine providence, the eternal law extends to all creatures. Among non-rational creatures, it is expressed through . . . intrinsic principles of operation, which are eternally contained in the Word of God but which work themselves out

in time and through the ordered movement of all creatures toward their appropriate ends. In this sense, all creatures may be said to be bound by the natural law. However, only the human person can consciously sin against the eternal law; non-rational creatures do not have sufficient freedom, whereas angels, who enjoy the supreme happiness of union with God, cannot choose to reject that happiness through sin.

The natural law is a temporal expression of the eternal law, as are all just (and therefore authentic) human laws. Within the human person, the natural law is grounded in reason; as such it is a reflection of the image of God within the human person, which Augustine equates with the rational soul. Hence, the natural law is innate, it is coeval with the creation of human beings, and it cannot be eradicated.[26]

One of the primary ways the medieval vision was expressed was in the belief in the necessity of monarchy, an understanding that was taken up in the politics developed after the Reformation. Society was to reflect heavenly order and required a directive principle that enabled it to achieve its true ends. Thus a city-state or nation was to be hierarchically structured, and the king was to rule for the common good. But the monarch is primarily the "chief magistrate" of the law, and his power is limited by the participation of others, natural equality, and the natural law.[27] Thus the monarchical principle can perhaps be realized in republican forms, as its effectiveness requires the realization of the collaborative "mixed polity" favored by classical and medieval political thinkers, with executive power residing in a presidential figure. The resistance to monarchal authority expressed in the American Revolution, as well as in the disestablishment of the church in the framing of the Constitution, illustrate the degree of departure from the comprehensive vision that operated even in the formation of the United States.

America: Two Steps beyond Christendom

Leaving aside the question of recent cultural developments, which surely move American and Western culture far from the medieval and Reformational formulations, the historical development of American government and society also worked to place the church in its current situation of displacement and dissociation. Many studies have charted this course, some approvingly and some disapprovingly, but it would be historically dishonest to blame the fragmentation faced at the beginning of the twenty-first century solely on the secularism of the twentieth century. America's origins may indeed have been as a collection of dispersed "cities on a hill," each seeking to form Jerusalem; but by the time of the framing of the Constitution, a different vision prevailed, even if it was built on an underlying understanding informed by the antecedents examined above. Even if America was a Christian society before the time of American independence, those who prevailed in the formation of the new government eschewed a fully Christianized polity as it had been understood until then.

These developments are not only bound up in the matter of nonestablishment (the refusal to declare a national church) but also in the decision to form a republic, and even more in the character of the society that emerged from the American colonies. Many of the new states emerging from the colonies maintained established churches into the early nineteenth century, though these eventually gave way to the prevailing ethos. Yet at its founding, America was at least two steps away from the medieval vision because of the influence of many developments since the days of the magisterial Reformation and the transfer of established churches from England to the New World. At least four shaping factors can be identified briefly, summarizing what has been fully explored by others.

1. The influence of the radical strains of the Reformation and the reaction to the corruptions of establishment, or Constantinianism. America became the home of many who fled the religious civil wars of Europe in the seventeenth century, especially the dissenters who—unlike the Puritans who fought to reform the national church along continental, Calvinist lines—sought total independence of the church. In the matter of governance, they departed from the view that the civil magistrate had both vocation from God and some degree of authority in church matters. These dissenters were persecuted in the colonies as they had been in England and elsewhere, but eventually they won acceptance—and even their own base in the case of Rhode Island. The cause of religious freedom became identified not only with toleration but, in America, with separation of religion from governance.

Roger Williams, founder of the colony in Rhode Island, stated most clearly the following convictions in 1644 as he sought investors in the new colony, describing its founding principles, radical at the time, but now commonplace in the United States:

- The doctrine of persecution for cause of conscience is proved guilty of all the blood of the souls crying for vengeance under the altar.
- All civil states with their officers of justice in their respective constitutions and administrations are proved essentially civil, and therefore not judges, governors, or defenders of the spiritual or Christian state and worship.
- It is the will and command of God that (since the coming of his Son the Lord Jesus) a permission of the most paganish, Jewish, Turkish, or anti-Christian consciences and worships be granted to all men in all nations and countries.
- The state of the land of Israel, the kings and people thereof in peace and war, is proved figurative and ceremonial; and no pattern nor precedent for any kingdom or civil state in the world to follow.
- God requireth not an uniformity of religion to be enacted and enforced in any civil state; which enforced uniformity (sooner or later) is the greatest occasion of civil war, ravishing of conscience . . . , and of the hypocrisy and destruction of millions of souls.
- An enforced uniformity of religion throughout a nation or civil state confounds the civil and religious, denies the principles of Christianity and civility, and that Jesus Christ is come in the flesh.[28]

By concentrating on the "cause of conscience," Williams made the primary issue for Christian political thinking one of personal belief and the right of association of intentional groups, and he dismissed the relevance of any communal realization of divine purposes in civil society. By challenging the constructive idea of "Jerusalem" as model and hope for civil society, he declared it to be God's will that the state be secular.

Skepticism about civil and ecclesiastical integration was a strong theme in America after its initial colonial period. John Adams described it as resistance to the "wicked confederacy between two systems of tyranny," through strict limits on the power of both church and state. Given this attitude, the strongest intellectual leaders of American disestablishment came from the regions with the longest and most deeply rooted traditions of church-state commonwealth: Jefferson and Madison in Virginia, John Adams in Massachusetts. The belief that any attempt to construct a form of Christendom, as the English and European forebearers had attempted to do, would lead to conflict and discrimination was deeply rooted. While many in the period of the framing of the new government expressed a general belief that "religion" was necessary to developing the virtues crucial to a self-governing republic and that God was to be honored, they could see no good in attempting to repeat the European experiments in Reformational Christendom.[29] It was a risky experiment in "ordered liberty," even of Christian order, that expected the sufficiency and strength of "religion" to sustain itself without political guidance, protection, or encouragement.[30]

   2. Religious pluralism as an American tradition. A major reason for not imposing a Christian structure on the new republic was the wide diversity in expressions of the church found among the colonies. From its beginnings, America was the recipient of many dissident groups seeking freedom, and it became the home of a bewildering array of religious and cultural minorities. Its later political unity was forged from its origins as a collection of disparate colonial establishments. In the mid-eighteenth century a German traveler, Gottlieb Mittelberger, noted about the mid Atlantic:

> Coming to speak of Pennsylvania again, that colony possesses great liberties above all other English colonies, inasmuch as all religious sects are tolerated there. We find there Lutherans, Reformed, Catholics, Quakers, Mennonists or Anabaptists, Herrnhuters or Moravian Brethren, Pietists, Seventh Day Baptists, Dunkers, Presbyterians, Newborn, Freemasons, Separatists, Freethinkers, Jews, Mohammedans, Pagans, Negroes, and Indians. The Evangelical and Reformed, however, are in the majority. But there are many hundred unbaptized souls that do not even wish to be baptized. Many pray neither in the morning nor in the evening, neither before nor after meals. No devotional book, not to speak of a Bible, will be found with such people. In one house and one family, four, five, and even six sects may be found.[31]

   This variety was expressed politically in the diversity of the groups that formed colonies and the churches that dominated those colonies, either officially or in effect. Anglicanism dominated in the southern colonies, Puritanism in New England, Catholicism in Maryland, but these colonies also received numerous members of dissenting sects, as well as non-English immigrants from across Europe. Yet the dominant political and social norm was that of the British Isles; perhaps the best depiction of America in its founding period is the way it translated and reproduced the growing religious pluralism of Britain after the Reformation period—developments that led to civil war and turmoil in the mother country.

When the new government of the United States was forged, it was necessary to support this experiment with a sense of nationhood and patriotism, detached from any loyalties to England or other nations of origin. Thus
John Jay, writing *Federalist #2* to urge ratification of the new Constitution
in 1789, could rise to some rhetorical hyperbole:

> It has often given me pleasure to observe that independent America was not
> composed of detached and distant territories, but that one connected, fer-
> tile, wide-spreading country was the portion of our western sons of liberty.
> . . . With equal pleasure I have as often taken notice that Providence has been
> pleased to give this one connected country to one united people—a people
> descended from the same language, professing the same religion, attached
> to the same principles of government, very similar in their manners and cus-
> toms, and who, by their joint counsels, arms, and efforts, fighting side by
> side throughout a long and bloody war, have nobly established their general
> liberty and independence. . . . This country and this people seem to have
> been made for each other, and it appears that it was the design of Providence
> that an inheritance so proper and convenient for a band of brethren, united
> to each other by the strongest ties, should never be split.[32]

This echoes the views of Edmund Burke, the great English parliamen-
tarian and political philosopher, who argued more subtly in his 1775
"Speech for Conciliation with the Colonies" that while a new national culture had developed in the colonies, it was yet a child true to its parentage:

> In this character of the Americans, a love of freedom is the predominating
> feature which marks and distinguishes the whole . . . and this from a great
> variety of powerful causes. . . . First, the people of the colonies are descen-
> dants of Englishmen. England, Sir, is a nation, which still I hope respects,
> and formerly adored, her freedom. The colonists emigrated from you when
> this part of your character was most predominant; and they took this bias
> and direction the moment they parted from your hands. They are therefore
> not only devoted to liberty, but to liberty according to English ideas, and on
> English principles.[33]

But Burke went on to argue that the economic, social, and political developments of America all worked toward the development of a national character enabling and requiring independence and diversity. This is reinforced
by American religion, according to Burke. "The people are Protestants; and

of that kind which is the most adverse to all implicit submission of mind and opinion. . . . All Protestantism, even the most cold and passive, is a sort of dissent."[34] Burke argued that all varieties of Protestantism practiced in the colonies, even Southern Anglicanism, pointed in their own ways to fierce defense of liberty, both from dominance by the government in London and against any imposed conformity. Thus Americans could be expected to form a system that would incorporate diversity and resistance to the integration of religious and national institutions, and especially resistance to any established or requisite conformity.

3. *The influence of the Enlightenment and Deism.* It is a common observation that by the time of the War of Independence and the formation of a national government, America was led by men whose ideas and experiences were shaped by the intellectual forces of the Enlightenment and whose religious beliefs were strongly influenced by Deism. Deism developed in the eighteenth century as a more "rational" religion, one which dismissed the miraculous, the providential intervention in history of a personal God, and the truth of revelation in favor of emphasis on the Creator of the structured order of nature, which could be perceived through rational processes. Charles Taylor, among many, has charted well the course of thought that leads to radical separation of faith and reason through the interaction of Deism and secular Enlightenment thinkers. Taylor stated that we should "take seriously the cliché that Deism is halfway on the road to the radical Enlightenment." In the Deist vision, the purpose of religion matches the purpose of the existence of community.

> God's goodness thus consists in his bringing about our good. His beneficence is explained partly in terms of our happiness. But what is striking about these Deist views is that the converse relation, so central to the religious tradition, seems to be lacking. It is after all a central tenet of the Judaeo-Christian religious tradition that God loves and seeks the good of his creatures. But this good in turn has always been defined as consisting in some relation to God: in our loving him, serving him, being in his presence, contemplating him in the beatific vision, or something of this kind.
>
> What is striking about Deist views is that the human good in terms of which God's benevolence is defined is so self-contained. It is not that the reference to God is wholly absent, but it seems to be subordinate to a conception of happiness which is defined purely in creaturely terms.[35]

The effect of Deism on the worldview of American elites was profound, enabling a concept of society and governance that gives priority to life, liberty, and "the pursuit of happiness." Is it too much to say that this is *not* the same as existing primarily for the glory of God and to see his will be done on earth as it is in heaven?

> The long slide from orthodox theologies of ordinary life to Deist visions of nature took place within this basic mould. The crucial activities are not identified by a vision of natural hierarchy, but they are marked by the purpose for which humans were made. Now, however, this is less and less a matter of God's inscrutable purposes which are shown to us in revelation, and more and more something we read off the design of nature itself. From this point of view, Deism does appear as a mere staging ground; at a later stage the design of nature itself will suffice to mark the activities of ordinary life.[36]

So the enlightened experiment of American formation sought to build a nation that emphasized natural liberty, but it also sought to apply all the lessons of the Enlightenment, especially as developed by Locke and Montesquieu, for the formation of a rational form of government. This government would have a symmetrical separation and balance of powers, clearly defined offices and responsibilities, and of course, as Article 6 of the Constitution requires, no religious test for qualification for governmental office in the United States.

4. *Commercialization and Industrialization.* Edmund Burke argued that following from their development of devotion to liberty "according to English ideas and English principles," Americans carried the English devotion to freedom of property and popular control of money to the shores of the New World. "Liberty inheres in some sensible object; and every nation has formed to itself some favourite point, which by way of eminence becomes the criterion of their happiness."[37] Following the long development of the control of taxation and freedom of property in England, through the evolution of the House of Commons, Americans took the principle to its fullest. Unlike the great "contests in the ancient commonwealths" that "turned primarily on the right of election of magistrates; or on the balance among the several orders of the state," the colonists followed the lead of their English ancestors.

They took infinite pains to inculcate, as a fundamental principle, that in all monarchies the people must in effect themselves, mediately or immediately, possess the power of granting their own money, or no shadow of liberty could subsist. The colonies draw from you, as with their life-blood, these ideas and principles. Their love of liberty, as with you, fixed and attached on this specific point of taxing.[38]

Charles Taylor has charted a larger pattern emerging in the West at the very time of the formation of America, especially in the English-speaking world, that had profound effect on the nature of American society. He echoes Burke in noting the "broad movements of the culture of the seventeenth and eighteenth centuries," including "the new value put on commercial activity and money-making."

The rise of this new valuation of commercial life can also be traced in the recession of the aristocratic honour ethic, which stressed glory won in military pursuits. Of course, this didn't come about without a struggle; and one of the crucial running controversies of the eighteenth century, at least in England, was this battle between two ethical outlooks. The "bourgeois" outlook stressed the goods of production, an ordered life, and peace—in short, accented the activities of ordinary life; the other stressed the virtues of the citizen life, of the search for fame and renown, and gave a central place to the warrior virtues.

In addition, the new science [of commercial life and economics] was grounded on the notion, utterly absent in previous ages, that the events in this domain form a self-regulating system. . . . The self-regulating system of production and exchange is a prime manifestation of the interlocking providential order of nature; it binds the productive, that is, those who follow the designated human vocation, into a mutually sustaining harmony.[39]

This new commercial order was not fully accepted in the new republic and was the source of early political battles such as those between Alexander Hamilton and Thomas Jefferson, and the conflict between the aristocratic and bourgeois visions explains much about the causes of the Civil War. It took many years for the Whig vision to win, but it was certainly an aspect of the founding motivations toward colonization and then independence. It seems reasonable to claim that much of the meaning of the American experiment is seen in the raising of prosperity and economic growth very high on the list of reasons for the creation and expansion of the new republic. Further, the idea that this system is self-regulating, not subject to norms derived from external authority, became a powerful shaping concept.

These observations do not seek to cast judgment on the development of the character of the American experiment. They serve to illustrate the degree to which it is in the character of American government and culture to move away from the comprehensive vision of the Christian commonwealth to another kind of vision. It was, to be sure, an experiment that extolled the centrality of religion, as in George Washington's famous claim: "Of all the dispositions and habits that lead to political prosperity, Religion and morality are indispensable supports. . . . Whatever may be conceded to the influence of refined education on the minds of peculiar structures, reason and experience both forbid us to expect that National morality can prevail in exclusion of religious principle." But it was not an experiment in comprehensive Christian public philosophy. It was the first of many experiments that followed in other nations—some much more radical, as in France—of rationalized and secularized society and politics, though one that took the formative role of religion as a central factor.

The Effects of Being beyond Christendom

> Perhaps it would be most accurate to describe the present relation of the churches to the American culture by saying not that we are living in a post-*Christian* era but rather that we are entering a post-*Christendom* era. . . . Christians . . . must abandon a long-held reliance on the culture to affirm biblical faith in crucial social and institutional contexts and to socialize individuals into something approximating a Christian way of life. . . . Commensurate with a crisis of Christian ethics is an interruption in the transmission of Christian tradition.[40]

Given both the long-term historical trends in America and the cultural developments of recent years, perhaps it is not a call for a new reformation that is appropriate, as is sounded from some quarters of the church. Such calls are anachronistic and presume that Christendom still exists and is to be reformed. The Reformation experiments sought to purify, purge, and reconstitute Christendom on a sounder basis. But in the current environ-

ment, there is nothing to re-form beyond the church itself. A full reformation in the historical sense, in the sense of those who advocate it, is of all
of culture, not just of the church.

All the experiments of Christendom, and in many ways the formation
of the American republic, were attempts at cultivating a godly order in a
fallen world. Often these experiments were defined as ways of living out
the life of "Jerusalem," with a godly king, true law, and right order among
citizens. All these experiments fell far short of these ideals and were subject
to violence, unlawfulness, and tyranny. Yet undergirding them was a sense
of universal divine order that could in some ways be reflected on earth
among humans in society.

Now we live in a culture not centered on such an understanding and in
need of reevangelization, a situation many have likened to that of the church
before Christendom. Thus many have called, as seen in the previous chapter, for formation projects. But we may be in a situation that requires much
earlier stages of formation, or "pre-formation." Given the full, comprehensive nature of a Christian society, and what seems to be the great dis-
tance between it and the situation of church now, the "pre-formation project" might be the most clearheaded notion of what the church must be
about in its calling to pray and work for God's will to be done on earth, as
it is in heaven.

3

The Search
for a Common Public Philosophy
in America

It is easy to see that no society could prosper without (dogmatic) beliefs, or rather that there are no societies which manage in that way. For without ideas in common, no common action would be possible, and without common action, men might exist, but there could be no body social. So for society to exist and, even more, for society to prosper, it is essential that all minds of the citizens should always be rallied and held together by some leading ideas; and that could never happen unless each of them sometimes came to draw his opinions from the same source and was ready to accept some beliefs ready made.

Alexis de Tocqueville, *Democracy in America*

This chapter will examine some of the outstanding general characteristics of American public culture, setting the stage for understanding the effects

of these trends on the church and for considering the agendas of those wanting to influence public life. These general characteristics reveal some of the
fault lines in the population, as well as some of the sources of unity still to
be found. The largely disconcerted quality of American public culture comes
through in the results of survey analyses, suggesting a troubled setting for
the public witness of the church in the coming decades. The extent to which
American culture is now shaped by values antagonistic to a healthy public
life, such as statism, privatization, and relativism, also poses challenges for
the church to consider in its approach to the shaping of public life.

Survey results also offer some clues to the impact of "faith-based" ideas
on public life and point to the effect of prevailing currents on religious institutions and their teachings. These data help us to understand the context
in which we ask: Can and should the church engage in a formative project
for public life?

Cautions are always in order when analyzing survey data, especially surveys that rely on self-reporting and examine beliefs and attitudes. Surveyors have learned that responses can be exaggerated or contradictory and
that even within a single survey similar questions can get contradictory
results. Respondents tend, for example, to overstate behaviors or attitudes
considered positive and to understate negatives. A good example is self-
reported voting patterns: up to 75 percent of people claim to have voted in
the last election, whereas turnout rates in recent years have actually been
50 percent or below. People may also report what they believe to be the
"correct" answer according to the value structure of their family, community, or personal convictions yet behave otherwise. For example, conservative Catholics and evangelicals may report in very high percentages that
"they always vote for the pro-life candidate," whereas in any given election
the votes of those groups may be split among the candidates because of the
personalities and other issues involved.

Survey researchers have learned to factor in these tendencies. The best
surveys are not quick opinion polls with a few questions, but those that are
longer and more thorough. Surveyors attempt to use neutral terminology,
to avoid leading questions, and to give no clues regarding "correct" answers.
They also seek to check answers by repeating questions or by asking different versions of the same question and then cross-tabulate the results to
gain a more accurate picture. The surveys employed in this book make use
of such sophisticated and qualifying approaches in efforts to gain more substantial and reliable information.[1] It is important to note, however, that the

contradictions and weaknesses explored in these pages may be partly explained by such problems in surveying and self-reporting. Survey data must always be interpreted according to a well-conceived framework and must be compared with other surveys, the insights of commentators, common sense, and one's own worldview.

Do Americans Have a Common Public Philosophy?

A common American public philosophy would offer a rationale for citizenship and give an account of the nature of American society. To meet the standards laid out by proponents, a common public philosophy should function in public culture to:

- articulate the connections between citizens and public life, placing individuals, families, and smaller communities in a larger context of commitment
- clarify the ideals and goals of public life and allow citizens to evaluate the achievement of those goals
- identify legitimate authority and enable citizens to affirm that authority in legitimate ways
- specify the nature of public responsibility and those who will undertake it
- provide for means of civic engagement by citizens

If the proponents of public philosophy are correct, a common body of commitments will produce a robust and healthy civic order. A general conclusion from many recent studies, however, points to an existing public culture (which changes slowly and will continue into the next decades) that in the aggregate (1) has detached private and personal expectations from public life, (2) is committed to traditional American political ideas but is skeptical about the delivery of those ideas by the political system, (3) resists and occasionally rejects authority and leadership, (4) lacks a clear idea about the responsibilities of government and citizenship, and (5) is civic-minded but not very engaged in civic life. It also is a culture that values individual rights and personal judgments more than the common good or shared moral commitments. Yet in general, this is a political culture that claims to hold religion in high importance and that exhibits few of the traits with which the media commonly portray it, such as victimization and economic anxiety. This moral-cultural diversity may explain some of the contentions in current political debate, the incommensurability of many political agendas, and the difficulty of achieving consensus in support of leadership and political direction.

Personal Destiny versus Common Destiny

Many surveys that seek to measure widely held perspectives indicate the high degree to which Americans on the whole express satisfaction with their personal circumstances: job, family, and community. Americans express personal satisfaction in high percentages and report low experience levels of the great tragedies that can profoundly affect families and individuals: natural disasters, serious crimes, accidents. They have high levels of positive expectation for their personal and family futures. Yet at the same time, high numbers of Americans express a sense of pessimism about the general state of America and seem to hold a strong belief that America is in decline. This is consistent with expressions of concern about decline in specific institutions and areas of cultural concern, such as public safety, public morals, family life, and education. Americans on the whole detach their personal and family destinies from the destiny of the nation.

Many surveys have asked Americans to describe their feelings about their current family life, job, church, and financial situation. In response, most Americans were very positive. In all cultural and economic categories, around 90 percent of Americans were pleased or enthused with their families, 75 to 80 percent were pleased with their current jobs, and similar percentages were pleased with their churches or fellowships. Eighty to 85 percent of all Americans were pleased with their overall spiritual condition. In the late 1990s, when asked about their financial situation, a minority of Americans (around 25 percent) indicated they were worried, but 65 percent were pleased or enthused. When asked about their expectations for their personal futures, one survey showed 34 percent were confused or worried, but 58 percent were pleased or enthusiastic.[2]

On matters that are traditionally understood to be at the heart of the concerns of religious moral teaching—spiritual life, family life, personal financial responsibility—Americans are generally satisfied and not inclined toward making major changes. In contrast, when asked about the general state of life in the United States, Americans are much less pleased and are more inclined to see serious problems. They see evidence of decline and are willing to detach their own destinies from the destiny of public life in the United States as currently constituted. They are not less supportive of the system or its ideals, as will be seen, but they see serious problems in the way American life is progressing.

More directly, when asked, "Do you think the United States is in decline, holding steady, or improving" as a nation, the belief in and expectation of decline stands out. Fifty-two percent perceived the United States to be in either strong or some decline, 40 percent believed the United States was holding steady, and only 9 percent perceived improvement. Further, when asked whether they were satisfied or dissatisfied with life in general in the United States, 41 percent were very or somewhat satisfied, and 58 percent were somewhat or very dissatisfied. Survey respondents also indicated they believe decline to be strong in many areas of American life, especially in family life, moral standards, public health and safety, education, entertainment and popular culture, quality of political leadership, and the criminal justice system. By contrast, Americans were roughly divided over whether they saw decline or improvement in the economy (with a slight edge to the holding steady/improving side), and a majority saw improvement or consistency in American military and global power and in the quality of religious institutions.

Thus it would seem that the gap between public and private destinies in the United States is widening. Most Americans are practiced in separating individual and family life from that of the nation as a whole. This may indicate to some a healthy independence from institutions and collectives, a traditional American resistance to standardization or submission. Yet it also demonstrates an embedded cultural willingness to minimize the ways in which public life affects private life. It perhaps also portends increasing separation of these realms and decreasing willingness to take political responsibility. This correlates with the relatively low levels of membership in civic and political groups (other than religious) and of general political participation. The thesis of Robert Putnam in his widely discussed article and book *Bowling Alone*,[3] that Americans are more detached from community life than ever before, gains some support from this interpretation.

The arenas in which Americans found greater encouragement—the military, business, and religious institutions—point to further detachment from overall political destiny, as their scores contrast drastically with the low confidence expressed in political and civic institutions. Individual and family life is not tied to the larger entity in our political culture. This perception points to other contradictions to be found in the American public, all of which suggest an increasingly precarious situation as support for the quality of public life in the United States erodes.

Ideals versus Practice

Another indicator of the contradictions in national life comes with the discovery that Americans on the whole demonstrate very high levels of adherence to the values, beliefs, and ideals that constitute the "American creed." The essential framework and structure of the American constitutional system is widely supported. The concepts of rights, self-government, equality, and democracy are supported by majorities in the 90 percent range. Overt demands for major systemic change or even revolution are minimal. Yet when asked about the current performance of the system and the credibility of its primary political institutions, Americans are much less supportive and much more critical. Many surveys reveal that trust and confidence in current government is very low. While some institutions get high marks for trust and performance, the national government does not. Such findings may portend demands in the near future for major changes in the political system of the United States, especially when Americans see indications that government institutions are not functioning well.

Large majorities of Americans were "proud to live under our system of government," believed "our system is the best possible system," and felt they "should support our system of government." These high numbers were true for all religious groups, in all regions, and among all age and ethnic groups. Americans also supported education about ways in which the United States has failed to live up to its ideals—which is another way of supporting those ideals and demonstrating the importance of the principles of equality and justice.

This spirit of criticism clearly extends to the level of trust in current institutions and national political leadership. In fact, the outlook on the current practitioners of politics is not very high. In survey responses, a majority of Americans agreed that

- "Our system of government is good, but the people running it are incompetent."
- "Our leaders are more concerned with managing their images than with solving our nation's problems."
- "People in government waste a lot of the money we pay in taxes."
- "Most politicians are more interested in winning elections than in doing what is right."

Beyond the view toward officeholders, however, responses to surveys indicate that Americans are also skeptical about the effectiveness of the political system as a whole. They are, as noted above, proud of the system and think it the best possible, but Americans are much more negative about whether the system is now capable of realizing those ideals. They sense that the system is not working well, and may even sense that it is not able to do so. We clearly live in a skeptical and suspicious age, and those suspicions are aimed at government and national leadership in strong ways. For example, 81 percent of respondents in one survey agreed that "our country is run by a close network of special interests, public officials, and the media." Sixty-three percent were willing to say that "the Federal government controls too much of our daily lives." When asked, "When the government in Washington decides to solve a problem, how much confidence do you have that the problem will actually be solved?" 60 percent responded that they had little or no confidence, 35 percent expressed some confidence, and only 4 percent expressed a lot of confidence. On the other hand, 60 percent of respondents agreed that "government often does a better job than people give it credit for."

Are Americans saying that their ideals still hold but that they seek different vessels or means to achieve those ideals? Does American government have to be "overhauled from the ground up," as former Speaker of the House Newt Gingrich put it? Is there a call for a new constitution? Or is this a rebuke, a call for better performance within established structures? In any case, this sentiment is a ringing challenge to the emerging relationship between citizens and the national government.

The attitude toward the national government contrasts with the confidence in and attitude toward local government. Majorities of Americans were pleased or enthusiastic about their local governments and expressed similar sentiments about local elected officials. Yet even these levels of trust, while majorities, are not overwhelming. The American system of differentiated powers has always held to the principle of preference for local institutions in matters that are closest to the immediate interests of citizens, and the accessibility of local government gives it certain advantages. These attitudes indicate that Americans are raising questions about the entire system in ways that may lead to demands for more significant changes—perhaps further devolution of responsibilities to the state and local level. Americans may also learn to demand greater accountability of their leaders, or they may demand different ways of selecting leaders altogether, along with stronger demands for national competence.

Anti-Elite Suspicions and Rejection of Leadership

A third strongly registered characteristic of Americans is the high level of suspicion of leaders in all categories. Surveys have questioned Americans about their perceptions of "the governing elite" regarding their patriotism, intentions, commitment to values, character, religion, and whether they were to be considered threatening or sympathetic. The elite were defined as those who run the government, the media, education, corporations, and other large institutions. While the level of negative perceptions of the elites was not as high as the negative perceptions specific to government, around 50 percent of Americans were suspicious of the elites.

For example, when Americans were asked to respond to a series of adjectives that might describe "America's governing elite," a mixed picture resulted. A majority said that the elite could be described well or very well as patriotic, well-meaning, and democratic. On the other hand, negative perceptions of the elite were high. Americans said that the following phrases described the elite not very well or not well at all: sensitive to the concerns of most Americans, religious, concerned about values and morality, concerned about the common good, concerned about the quality of life, people of conviction, mainstream, people of character. Respondents also said the elite could be described as out of touch with reality, hypocritical, and only concerned about their own agenda. However, respondents rejected the most damaging depictions; views that elites pose a threat to society or that they are backward, mean-spirited, extremist, or involved in a conspiracy tend to be overwhelmingly rejected in the 75 percent range.

Of course, Americans have always expressed some level of skepticism about politicians and the powerful. American constitutional structure places limits on power and assumes that political leadership will be checked by public will. Antipolitical attitudes have been mainstays of the American scene, from the Anti-Federalists to Jacksonian democrats to William Jennings Bryan's Populism to Huey Long to Pat Buchanan. It is an American tradition to question and put checks upon the intentions of corporate leaders and those who control large institutions. But the background to skepticism about power has been a vigorous civil society and the confidence in local community, family, personal ability, and economic success necessary to full life and happiness. Sustaining such confidence has been a deep sense of trust that what one has been taught and raised with, in family and school and church, is right and can sustain life even in adversity. If that sense of trust is now eroding, a question examined later, then there is little confidence left in any public authority in the American project.

Perhaps this loss of legitimate authority helps explain why so many Americans (up to 80 percent in some surveys) are willing to accept conspiracy theories about power—for example, "Our country is run by a close network of special interests, public officials, and the media"—and why as many as 25 percent of the public believe that the phrase "involved in conspiracy" describes the governing elite well. The embattlement at the core level of value and belief yields a multitude of popular theories about "why things seem so good when they really are rotten."

Does this suspicion extend to an erosion of the authority of church leadership? Public scandals involving religious leaders in the past decades might lead to that expectation. Further, the high level of individualism and the low level of trust in institutional norms or the guidance of authority figures, as seen in survey results, suggest that religious leaders also have little real authority. On the other hand, prominent religious leaders (Billy Graham, the pope) are among the public figures for whom Americans showed the highest levels of admiration. Of course, Oprah Winfrey also ranked on par with these figures. Religious leaders, then, still exercise some cultural influence, perhaps as moral examples, and in light of the high levels of religious participation and identity among the American public, religious leaders may stand out as those with the greatest possibility for influence even in this period of high skepticism about leadership.

As they begin the twenty-first century, Americans are concerned—as shown in their views of national decline, their low levels of confidence in political institutions, and their views of leaders—primarily for the moral and community challenges facing the United States. Crime, family life, and moral standards are the areas of greatest concern; this joins the sense that leaders care little for the concerns and problems of the American people to suggest that the gap in moral leadership is the outstanding political problem facing American leaders. The legitimacy of leadership and authority is very low because of this. Church leaders considering their role in the formative project will see that their "specialty" is at the center of concerns leading to declining trust in American public culture.

Table 3.1

Do you completely agree, mostly agree, mostly disagree, or completely disagree that:

	Completely agree %	Mostly agree %	Mostly disagree %	Completely disagree %
Most elected officials don't care what people like you think	19	50	26	5
Our system of government is good, but the people running it are incompetent	16	50	30	4
Our leaders are more concerned with managing their own images than with solving the nation's problems	30	48	19	3
People in government waste a lot of the money we pay in taxes	49	42	7	2
The government is run by a few big interests looking out for themselves	31	50	17	3
Political events these days seem more like theater or entertainment than like something serious	30	50	17	3
Our country is run by a close network of special interests, public officials, and the media	26	55	15	3
The federal government controls too much of our daily lives	23	40	31	7
People like you don't have any say about what the government does	18	42	30	10
So many other people vote in national elections that it doesn't matter much whether you vote or not	9	18	33	40
The way the government is running, a government shutdown probably does more good than harm	10	23	35	32
Most politicians are more interested in winning elections than in doing what is right	28	51	17	4
The federal government seems mostly hostile to religion	11	29	43	18
Our federal tax system is basically unfair	25	43	27	6
The best government is one that governs the least	20	41	29	10
Government often does a better job than people give it credit for	10	50	31	9

Beliefs about Public and Political Responsibility

In spite of the suspicion of elites and the low confidence in government, Americans still have high expectations of the national government and a sense that government has major responsibilities in all aspects of life. President Clinton proclaimed in his 1996 State of the Union address that "the era of big government is over." But Americans still want to view the state as a major, perhaps even the primary, institution in American life. The general view of Americans regarding public responsibility is essentially statist.

Some advocates have claimed that many public problems are not federal government responsibilities and should be left to individual, private, or local responsibility. Yet Americans still believe that the federal government has the primary responsibility for protecting the environment (65 percent), enforcing fair treatment of minorities (67 percent), upholding health standards for agricultural products (70 percent), and financing health care (63 percent). These statistics join the expected view of 91 percent of Americans that the federal government has primary responsibility for national security.

Another measurable set of attitudes is whether Americans see private organizations or individuals as primarily responsible for certain public concerns. The highest nongovernmental expectation was for financing a college education, yet that was seen as a private responsibility by only 30 percent of Americans. Such questions represent a wide range of public issues and can be used to test Americans' understanding of public responsibility. As the chart indicates, Americans have high expectations of national and state governments.

Table 3.2

Should the following public concerns be mainly the responsibility of the federal government, state government, local government, private organizations, or individuals (in percentages of all Americans)?

Issue	Federal Govt.	State Govt.	Local Govt.	Private Orgs.	Individuals
Protect environment	65	20	7	4	5
Fair treatment of women and minorities	67	18	7	3	5
Health standards for meat and dairy products	70	21	6	2	1
National security	91	6	3	1	0
Help poor and unemployed	40	38	14	4	3
Finance college education	28	27	7	9	30

continued

Issue	Federal Govt.	State Govt.	Local Govt.	Private Orgs.	Individuals
Guard against hiring discrimination	53	29	11	5	3
Setting workplace safety standards	51	30	12	5	2
Decide when school prayer is permissible	28	23	23	3	24
Setting educational standards	32	43	19	2	4
Permitting smoking in public places	26	25	29	6	15
Feeding poorest Americans	58	20	14	5	4
Financing health care	63	19	5	5	9
Mean	51.7	24.5	12	4	8

Calculating the mean of these responses shows that government is the institution felt to be primarily responsible for public problems. On an informal "statism scale" drawn from averaging these responses, Americans give weight to government in high proportions: 51.7 percent to the federal government alone, 76.2 percent to federal and state governments combined, 88.3 percent to all governments combined. Within all of the categories, the combined responses given to governments garner large majorities.

These high expectations may explain in part why the public is disappointed in and has low confidence in government and its leaders, yet the findings also reflect the degree to which an undifferentiated public philos-

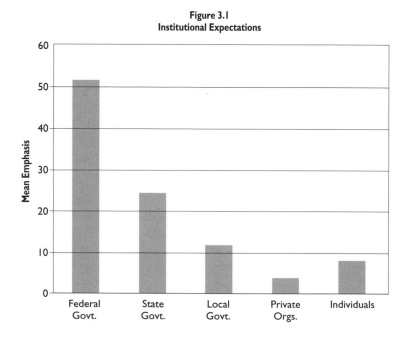

Figure 3.1
Institutional Expectations

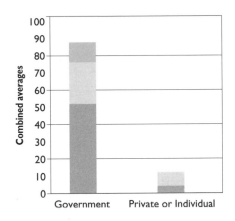

Figure 3.2
Government or Non-Government?

ophy still holds in the United States. Not only the more conservative policy agendas that seek to shift power away from the national government in
Washington but also those who see the importance of a commitment to
civil society and its mediating institutions have much work to do. Finally,
it is clear that Americans understand federalism—the division of powers
among different levels of government—but they do not have a strong concept of differentiated responsibilities to the institutions of civil society.
Americans' understanding of public responsibility is one of simple statism.
Hope for robust civil society is not to be found in the general public understanding; however, there may be a gap between these survey findings and
the actual strength and activity of public institutions, as well as citizen confidence in specific institutions.

Confidence and Participation in Mediating Institutions

In this situation of cultural statism, Americans tend to rate their trust in
other institutions only slightly higher than that given to government. While
they say that government should undertake the various responsibilities indicated in the previous section, 51 percent have only some confidence and
18 percent have very little confidence in the national government. With
low confidence in government, Americans might then be expected to have
greater trust in other types of public organization. But similar levels of uncer-

tainty are also shown in questions about other institutions. It seems that all established institutional patterns are under tough scrutiny.

This atmosphere of uncertainty is notable in regard to the family, which we might expect to have higher trust levels, given that a large group of Americans (up to 90 percent) are pleased or enthused with their own family life. Yet about 60 percent are worried or concerned about the institution of the family to some degree, and only 25 percent are pleased or enthusiastic with the state of families in general. Fifty-four percent of Americans are also worried about public schools, and only 28 percent are pleased. Fifty-six percent are worried about the economy, while 20 percent are pleased or enthusiastic, though 76 percent express contentment with their current jobs and 65 percent are happy with their personal financial situation.

Organized religion fares better than governmental institutions and stands out as the institution receiving the highest measures of confidence. Sixty-four percent have a great deal or quite a lot of confidence in religion. Along with the finding that 88 percent of Americans say religion is very or fairly important to them, religious institutions are among the most significant influences in American life. Yet this confidence has soft spots, as will be shown later.

Finally, the participation of Americans in the organizations of civil society is relatively low. With the exception of church (54 percent of all Americans) and church-affiliated groups (14 percent) and health (13 percent) and sports (12 percent) organizations, Americans are not joiners. Less than 10 percent are involved in civic, political, professional, and other organizations.

Table 3.3

To what types of clubs or organizations do you belong?

Category	% of All Americans
Fraternal groups	6
Civic organizations	8
Veterans organizations	6
Environmental/nature	5
Labor unions	9
Sports clubs	12
Youth clubs	7
School service (e.g., PTA)	10
Health or fitness	13
Hobby or garden clubs	7

School fraternity/sorority	4
Nationality organizations	2
Farm organizations	2
Art, literary, or music organizations	6
Discussion/study groups	5
Professional or academic societies	9
Ethnic or racial organizations	1
Church/temple/mosque	54
Church-affiliated or religious organization	14
Consumer group/buying club	7
Therapeutic or counseling group	3
Other	7

It seems that Americans at the end of the twentieth century have big question marks about all of the key institutions of public culture and decreasing confidence in their survival. Thus while some political leaders and many theorists want to roll back the power of the national government and give greater power and responsibility to local governments and other institutions, the expectations of the American people still show another way of thinking. Education, public discourse, and the hard realities of declining national power may change this mind-set, but it will take time. In the meantime, low confidence in all public institutions, along with the trend toward privatization and withdrawal from public life, suggests an ambivalent public culture that may be ripe for upheaval. Any formative project will have to account for the weakness of these institutions and find ways of encouraging multiple forms of responsibility.

An Age of Fragmentation

An effective and comprehensive public philosophy must have clarity in the elements tested in this chapter: commitment to the common good and the common destiny of the nation; commitments to core ideals and confidence they can be largely realized; legitimization of authority and trust in leadership; clarity about who has public responsibilities; and strength and coordination among the formative institutions of society. Fluidity and even weakness in all these areas is clear from survey results. Tocqueville's warning about the need for common ideas sounds an alarm in this environment.

Canadian political philosopher Charles Taylor has decried the fragmentation and detachment he discerns in North American society: "A fragmented society is one whose members find it harder and harder to identify with their political society as a community . . . because the absence of effective common action throws people back on themselves" and increases social fragmentation.[4] Commenting on Taylor's concerns, Jean Bethke Elshtain notes that fragmentation leads to cynicism. "This growing cynicism about politics promotes a spiral of delegitimation . . . Over time, the 'culture of mistrust' grows, aided by public scandals and selfish individualism."[5]

Elshtain calls for a solution to this fragmentation and spiral of mistrust and cynicism in the form of a "new social covenant." She warns that this will not be easy

> unless Americans, or the citizens of any faltering democracy, can once again be shown that they are all in it together; unless democratic citizens remember that being a citizen is a civic identity, not primarily a private sinecure; unless government can find a way to respond to people's deepest concerns, a new democratic social covenant has precious little chance of taking hold . . . . The social covenant is not a dream of unanimity or harmony, but the name given to a hope that we can draw on what we hold in common even as we disagree.[6]

It is apparent from the analysis of survey data that the American public does not hold much of a common public philosophy. Some of its elements are still to be found, but such a framework does not permeate public life in the way proponents of comprehensive common ground in the form of a social covenant would advocate. Yet it could be that while a public philosophy does not hold the American people together, other things are still held in common. The next chapter will attempt to measure whether underneath the fragmentation some solid ground can be discerned, whether some common moral or political commitments might yet provide a base for the formation of a legitimizing public philosophy. Unfortunately, even digging to this deeper level uncovers shifting sands.

4

The Search for Common Identity, Morality, and Political Goals in America

Augustine criticizes Cicero's definition of a *res publica* as an association based on common agreement concerning right and on shared interests. Within the terms of this definition, Rome was never a true commonwealth. But Cicero's definition itself is wanting. A people is a gathering or multitude of rational beings united in fellowship by sharing a common love of the same things. Using this definition, we can not only define what a society is, but we can also determine what it is that people hold dear.

Jean Bethke Elshtain, *Augustine and the Limits of Politics*

In this time of political contradiction and uncertainty, and of fragmenting support for institutions and leaders, underlying cultural patterns have an amplified effect on public life. They are not masked by institutional iner-

tia or official traditions. "What a people holds dear" may be even more evident in times of disaffiliation. Yet even in times of consensus, expectations
for political institutions and the beliefs that guide policymaking come from
somewhere: from the demands and needs of a public guided by the systems
of values that predominate. Political leaders and policy goals will be shaped,
at least in part, by the demands prevailing in the culture.

Thus in the absence of a clearly grasped and widely held public philosophy, it could be possible to discover in America some rudimentary public commonality in an underpinning moral framework or in a few widely
approved public goals. These could, if they exist, then provide the basis for
the reconstruction of a common vision of public life. Many analysts, from
Alexis de Tocqueville to the present, have argued that democracy requires
a substantial body of moral underpinnings, derived from religion, in order
for a people to be self-governing.

> Despotism may be able to do without faith, but freedom cannot. Religion
> is much more needed in the republic . . . and in democratic republics most
> of all. How could society escape destruction if, when political ties are relaxed,
> moral ties are not tightened? And what can be done with a people master of
> itself if it is not subject to God?[1]

Many contemporaries hold out the hope that this basic morality will flour-
ish even in the midst of political turmoil and will be a source of responsible citizenship and leadership.

It is worth exploring, then, whether it is possible to find indicators in
the American public of widely affirmed foundational frameworks that
could establish principles and lay out moral boundaries. How do Americans determine their support for policy or other aspects of public life? How
are the evaluations of government and leadership seen in the previous chapter formulated? On what basis do Americans determine that leaders are
falling short, that government is not doing its job, that public life is in
decline? Are some shared, fundamental values discernible in American
public culture?

The answer, in this case as well as in that of public philosophy, presents
a very confused picture; the contradictions found in public evaluations
come not from common beliefs and consistent evaluations but from conflicting values and frameworks found within the public. In general, it can
be said that there is little evidence for a broad common moral framework

out of which the American people aim at common ends. This leads to the discovery that there are multiple contending moral and cultural frameworks, and consequent public philosophies, at work in the United States today. These contending systems form the fault lines for current political battles and for any future conflicts that may emerge as the United States deals with the cultural and political stresses arising at the beginning of the twenty-first century.

Sources of Moral and Ethical Determinations

Survey data can be examined to explore how Americans make decisions about a number of private and public concerns, and what commitments guide those decisions. The results reveal the moral frameworks and attitudes underlying the public perspectives discussed earlier by identifying three apparently contradictory trends in the American public: (1) dual adherence to relativism and to absolute standards, (2) dual commitment to individual freedom and to the common good, and (3) incompatible goals for public life.

Dual Adherence to Relativism and to Absolute Standards

The American public strongly affirms both moral systems that acknowledge absolute standards based on the will of God and those that give great freedom to the individual to determine what is right. Along with the tendency of all survey respondents to give contradictory answers to such questions, this finding can be explained in part by the differences between identified groups; for example, secularists are more likely to hold to relativism, while evangelicals and traditional Catholics are more likely to express belief in absolutes. But the high level of responses to both orientations cannot be explained by this factor alone, suggesting that many Americans find both relativism and absolute standards compelling. Further, the same contradictions can be found within the groups that might be expected to be more consistent.

These tendencies are seen in responses to survey questions about moral decision making. When asked in one survey, "If you were unsure of what was right or wrong, which would be the most important in deciding what you would do?" 49 percent of Americans answered, "Doing what would be best for everyone involved," and 26 percent responded, "Doing what God or Scripture tells you is right." Other possible answers, each receiving 10 percent or less, were personal happiness (10 percent), getting ahead (8 percent), or following expert advice (7 percent). This tendency was seen in all groups, with the exception of evangelicals, who answered 57 percent for following God or Scripture. At the same time, 85 to 90 percent of Americans indicate some level of belief that the Bible is the Word of God, and well over 90 percent believe there is a God or some ruling spirit. These responses by themselves would suggest the operation of absolute standards or guiding principles at work in American culture.[2]

The picture becomes less clear, however, when respondents were asked to indicate how they actually make decisions, and what sources of morality they consult. While 70 percent agreed that "those who violate God's rules will be punished," and 75 percent agreed that "we would all be better off if we could live by the same basic moral guidelines," Americans still seem to think they are on their own in determining right and wrong.

- Eighty-five percent completely or mostly agreed that "values are something that each of us must decide without being influenced by others."
- Over 90 percent agreed to some degree that "what is true for me is not necessarily true for others."
- Nearly 60 percent agreed to some measure that "all views of what is good are equally valid."

On the other hand, 58 percent disagreed, and only 38 percent agreed, that "it's hard to know right from wrong, because the answers change from year to year." *Americans, it can be concluded, are in general confident about their own individual moral perceptions but are not willing to hold their fellow citizens to a common moral framework.*

As in matters of public philosophy, Americans tend to take a very personalized approach to moral questions. We are very confident about our own judgments but hesitant to apply them to others. Further, we hesitate to accept that a source of common morality can be defined authoritatively. While belief in God is strong, we find it difficult to apply even this general affirmation to public questions. It is no wonder that we have difficulty agreeing on evaluations of or appropriate responses to the behavior of public officials, or on a multitude of other questions that are presented in daily public life.

These findings are highly ambiguous, and they are the kind of results that can be used in part to support any assertion. Both those who hope for high levels of belief in absolute standards and those who are concerned about relativism will find ample evidence among Americans. The overall picture is of ambiguous and personalized moral decision making. There is no widespread agreement in principle on a general moral approach or framework. This does not mean, necessarily, that Americans disagree on the actual judgments they make together on tough questions. Thus a better test of commonality is to consider whether common assumptions are *actually* held and *operatively* employed when specific judgments are called for, which will be explored in our discussion of incompatible goals for public life.

Dual Commitment to Individual Freedom and to the Public Good

As in the patterns regarding relativism and absolute standards, the American public generally shows dual commitment to both individual freedom and to the public good. Strong support for each emphasis can be found, even when they seem to contradict.

When asked, "When you compare the importance of individual freedom and the public good, which takes priority in your mind?" American responses broke down roughly along these lines:

- 17 percent said that individual freedom took greater or much greater priority
- 34 percent said that the public good was greater or much greater
- 49 percent said that they gave equal priority to these values

On one side of this dichotomy, Americans express at very high levels the conviction that they have certain public obligations that transcend personal preference. And when asked whether individual freedom or the public good has greater priority in a variety of situations (smoking in public, carrying weapons, cheating on taxes, burning the flag, paying minimum wage to employees), they chose the public good in far greater numbers.

Table 4.1

When you compare the importance of individual freedom (IF) and the public good (PG), which takes priority in your mind?

	(1) IF much greater (2) IF greater (3) Equal priority of IF and PG (4) PG greater (5) PG much greater in percentages of all Americans				
Category	**(1)**	**(2)**	**(3)**	**(4)**	**(5)**
General	7	10	49	25	9
When a person wants to:					
Smoke in public	7	8	21	36	28
As a business owner, ignore minimum wage laws	7	10	16	31	36
Carry an unlicensed concealed weapon	5	6	9	26	55
Sell a record that glamorizes violence against women	4	7	15	25	50
Not report tips for tax purposes if waitress	11	14	24	30	22
Burn the U.S. flag to demonstrate frustration with the government	8	12	15	22	44

Americans tend to report that their civic participation is very high, even though actual measures do not support these assertions. When asked whether they voted in the last election, around 75 percent said they had, though actual turnout was around 50 percent. When asked, "How interested are you in politics and national affairs?" 27 percent said they were very interested, 43 percent were somewhat interested, 22 percent were slightly interested, and 9 percent were not interested at all. These responses were among the few that varied widely across education levels and social class, with higher education and income correlating to higher interest levels.

These responses have to be compared, however, with the actual levels of participation in and support for the institutions of community. As already seen, this is much lower than the expressions of verbal support might suggest. Americans have a strong sentiment for community but do not easily reconcile that with other demands. Further, these answers also contrast with the American insistence that personal judgment must be exercised in specific situations even if community norms are clearly understood. When asked to respond to the comment, "Being true to myself is the best way of furthering the public good," as high as 80 percent of Americans completely or mostly agreed. For most Americans, then, the common good is defined as an aggregation of individual interests.

Given the strong commitment to both individual freedom and to the public good, policies successfully implemented in this climate will be those in which both interests converge, where a large majority of individual interests and community interests run on similar paths. These will be rare cases. It is hard to predict in such a climate whether Americans will sacrifice individual interests to a larger good if called upon to do so. A serious crisis may prove otherwise, but in the normal course of events, one might wonder if Americans are actually inclined toward the common good. In light of the demonstrated perception of national decline and the lack of public trust shown in many studies, the high level of sentiment for community may remain unrealized in practice. Americans clearly desire to have a strong community life, but they are reluctant to say that the existing national form of community meets that desire. Perhaps only a clear sense of public purpose, and leadership that unifies and directs that purpose, can restore true community. As a source of moral guidance, however, these orientations now remain in conflict.

Incompatible Goals for Public Life

Since Americans are not in agreement about the sources of a moral framework for public life and reserve moral judgments for themselves as individuals, is it yet possible to find some firm common ground in their actual judgments made about common concerns? Americans do express in large proportions the belief that as citizens they have certain public obligations, such as reporting crimes, volunteering for community service, donating blood and organs, voting, being civil in public, being informed on public issues, and working to reduce inequality. The positive response to these civic sentiments shows that Americans on the whole have some sense of common public responsibilities, at least as general propositions regarding actual issues.

However, when surveys test beliefs on a range of issues that have direct impact on public behavior and on policy—examining whether the general sense of obligations to the common good would be expressed in more concrete terms as commonly understood standards—the picture is very different. For example, when one survey questioned whether Americans would fight for their country, 31 percent said they would under any condition, while 12 percent said they would not fight at all. Forty-eight percent indicated they would reserve judgment and fight only under some conditions, a finding almost identical to that which shows Americans hold community and individual interests as equivalent.

Another area explored was whether Americans commonly held certain public concerns to be "wrong for all," "right for all," or subject to more personal judgments such as "wrong for me, but right for others," or "wrong, but should be legally tolerated." Questions on public tolerance and intolerance, and the degree to which Americans are willing to apply the force of law to these practices, give good indicators on the level of commitment to common standards. These data also confirm the American tendency to give high place to personal choice and to tolerance even of things that are considered wrong. Only two matters tend to be considered by the majority of Americans to be wrong and deserving to be illegal: cheating on taxes (65 to 70 percent) and smoking marijuana (about 51 percent). On all other concerns questioned, even those a majority of Americans considered wrong (homosexual marriage, homosexual activity, pornography, infidelity, slander, public swearing, revenge), the majority were not willing to apply legal sanctions to those practices. For the majority of these concerns, the strongest answers were either "wrong, but should be legally tolerated" or "right for some, but not for me personally." Again, Americans are willing on the whole to make moral determinations, but they are very reluctant to insist that those judgments are held in common or that they are to be applied throughout the culture.

Table 4.2

How wrong do you personally think it is when people engage in the following behavior?

	Wrong for all, should not be legally tolerated	Wrong for all, but should be legally tolerated	Right for some, but not for me personally	Right for me, but nor necessarily for others	Right for all	Not a moral issue
Cheating on taxes	68%	11%	10%	3%	2%	7%
Smoking marijuana	51	13	19	4	3	10
Marriages between two persons of the same sex	41	19	24	3	4	10
Sexual relations between two adults of the same sex	33	23	27	3	5	10
Watching pornography	39	17	26	6	3	8
Failing to follow through on commitment	23	33	21	4	3	15
Making negative remarks about someone not present	22	33	21	4	3	18

Swearing or using offensive language	22	33	22	6	4	14
Mistreating someone who mistreated you	26	27	26	5	5	12
Abortion during first three months of pregnancy	34	16	24	6	11	8
Medically assisted suicide for someone terminally ill	32	13	26	9	13	7
Sex before marriage	16	27	22	15	9	11
Smoking cigarettes	13	19	30	13	8	18
Withdrawing life support if someone requests it	16	12	23	14	28	8
Marriage between blacks and whites	13	13	39	5	15	17
Drinking alcohol	11	14	29	17	10	18
Divorce	5	18	42	10	13	12
Spanking a child	10	11	24	19	20	16
Suing someone who has wronged you	8	12	27	10	28	15
Accepting welfare payment from the government	7	12	45	6	14	16

Finally, it is significant that many of these areas show rising levels of tolerance for practices that have been illegal or that have received strong disapproval in the past. And some of the practices that rouse the moral concerns of conservative or religious groups—such as abortion, pornography, divorce, premarital sex, medical termination of life—are widely tolerated by the general population.

These indicators of shifting moral perspectives, along with the tendency of Americans to respond positively to all approaches of moral decision making, indicate more confusion than clarity in American public culture. Surely the postmodern trends charted by many analysts are apparent in American life—especially the beliefs that logical consistency is impossible and that values are determined by experience and heritage or imposed by the powerful, rather than derived from absolute sources. Americans on the whole seem comfortable with the softness and relativity of central values.

Many cultural and political effects of these phenomena are showing up in public and political life and will be explored later.

- These data confirm the observation of many that American public values are shifting and that the culture as a whole is at odds with some goals advanced by activist groups. For example, Americans in surveys across the board approved changes in the role of women, more public openness about sex, greater ethnic and cultural diversity, greater acceptance of divorce, and the popular focus on health and fitness. On the other hand, they also approved "more willingness to question the authority of government," again suggesting support for agendas that are challenging the legitimacy of the United States government. An important exception to the general approval of changes was greater acceptance of homosexuality: just under 50 percent think this is mostly or very good; just over 50 percent think it mostly or very bad. Yet even this is much higher acceptance than in the past and shows a nearly even division in the public.

- The tendency of Americans to approve just about any moral system and to support both absolute standards and individual choice gives little solid ground on which issue advocates and policymakers can make their case to the American people. Very little can be taken for granted. Each policy initiative or advocated position has to be argued from scratch rather than from appeal to accepted principles. The decline of common assumptions at fundamental levels suggests that the type of political experience wherein even the simplest policy developments are highly contested on the basis of group interest will be a part of the American scene for years. And pragmatic, consensus-building approaches are more likely to win than principled approaches.

- The high level of frustration with political life and the generalized perceptions of decline may be based not on clear standards and disappointments but rather on the vagueness of definition of our common life. Americans at the beginning of the twenty-first century were generally prosperous and secure; the economy was up, crime was down, no wars were threatening prior to September 11, 2001. So if Americans exhibited "the strange melancholy often haunting inhabitants of democracies in the midst of abundance, . . . that disgust with life sometimes gripping them in calm and easy circumstances,"[3] perhaps it is because collectively we do not know what public life should be about.

Common Political Goals

Since little in the way of common public philosophy or underlying moral frameworks can be found in the United States as a whole, a further question worth raising is whether some common political goals might be found that provide a level of minimal agreement on public life. Major surveys have examined the views of the American people on a number of specific issues to see how the identified patterns of political culture find their way into specific policy preferences. For a pragmatic people, consensus on processes and issues might have to perform the role otherwise taken by a philosophical and moral consensus on the purpose and meaning of public life. Survey analysis has sought to discern what long-term political directions might be indicated by responses on the following matters:

Table 4.3

How much do you favor or oppose the following?

	Favor	Neutral	Oppose
Guaranteeing every American adequate medical care, whether or not they can pay for it	81%	8%	11%
Balancing the federal budget	73	16	8
Making English the official language of the United States	73	12	10
The death penalty for persons convicted of murder	67	14	18
Setting term limits for members of Congress	66	18	14
Allowing voluntary prayer in public schools	65	18	14
Reducing the size of the federal government	64	21	11
Passing stronger restrictions on the sale and use of handguns	63	12	23
Reducing the size of state governments	57	25	15
Shifting many government functions from the federal level to the states	57	21	18
Increasing government spending on prisons and law enforcement	52	20	27
Passing stronger restrictions against smoking in public places	50	20	25
Allowing gays to serve in the military	38	22	35
Increasing defense spending	36	27	36
Ending affirmative action programs for women and minorities	35	23	39
Reducing federal regulations aimed at protecting the environment	34	19	45
Using American soldiers to keep peace in the Balkans	32	21	46
Reducing welfare payments to persons living in poverty	31	20	48
Increasing foreign aid to impoverished nations	29	27	44

A Gallup poll released on November 1, 2000, just before the presidential election, showed a voting public quite divided on leading issues. Gallup concluded that the "results of this referendum process show once again the difficulty of attempting to assign broad labels to the American population. The people have decidedly mixed views overall, and the results show that over two-thirds of the American people say they would vote 'for' both a number of what could be considered traditionally conservative issues, as well as what could be considered liberal propositions."[4] The study shows large numbers of Americans favor a raise in the minimum wage, handgun control, and legal abortion, as well as favoring prayer in public schools, privatization of Social Security, and reduction in the size of government.

Consistent with earlier observations, other survey results show strong support for mild reform policies that limit or challenge the power of entrenched leadership and that seek to reduce national government power, for example, a balanced budget amendment to the Constitution, term limits for members of Congress, and "reducing the size of government." Little support is shown for strong initiatives in foreign policy—an area primarily controlled by the national government—such as increasing foreign aid, using force in the Balkans, increasing military capabilities. However, also consistent with the findings that Americans have strong expectations for the national government are the desires of Americans for programs in health care, environmental protection, and job security. The observation that it seems typical of Americans to want contradictory outcomes (smaller government but bigger programs) gains validity when viewing responses to specific issue questions. Americans seem to have difficulty relating their specific demands to larger political philosophy or strategies. The manifest dissatisfaction of Americans toward their political system seems to flow from both unfulfilled expectations and the uncertainty over a moral and philosophical vision for the political system. Yet the political deadlock this leads to only furthers the sense of frustration and dissatisfaction with the competence of the political system.

Public Identity

Finally, it is worth exploring how Americans identify themselves and others when asked to describe the most important factors in public life. If Americans agree in general on some common needs or share common experiences, this might also point to sources of common public concern or expectation. As Elshtain puts it, a people is identified by what it holds dear. What personal demands are most significant in forming the basis on which Americans evaluate public life? Further, what general characterizations can be made of the experiences and patterns that can become the basis for both public policy responses and media portrayals of the American public? Politics is sometimes portrayed as a common effort against widespread problems: poverty, disease, natural disaster, psychological challenges, discrimination, and so on. As shown earlier, Americans did agree that adequate medical care seems to be a cause most Americans rally around. But are Americans as unhappy, victimized, racially conscious, secular, and amoral as they often are portrayed?

Survey results indicate that according to some of the ways Americans perceive themselves, even consensus on common needs or services is shallow.

- Americans in general do not seem to see race or sex as very significant factors in political life. Nor is this the case with ethnic identity or age. As seen in other areas, Americans claim that individual identity overrides any of these external characteristics. Those who advocate gender- or race-based public life have only minority support in the United States.

Table 4.4

How much do you agree with the following?
(percentages of all Americans)

	Completely agree	Mostly agree	Mostly disagree	Completely disagree	Don't know
How a person thinks about political issues is mostly a function of gender.					
	5	24	37	27	8
People of other races can't really understand the way my race sees things.					
	10	29	34	21	7
Being true to myself is the best way of furthering the public good.					
	30	49	12	4	6
The average American doesn't have the education and background to make responsible choices about political matters.					
	5	22	39	29	5
You can usually predict someone's political views by their generation.					
	5	30	36	23	7
A person's ethnic or group identity is more important than the things they say.					
	4	17	35	38	8

- Americans are not only committed to the priority of their families, as we have seen, but in great numbers are very satisfied with their families. Over 90 percent rate their ties to family and friends as strong and 75 percent as "close." Few Americans report that their own families are in the serious state of decline that some pro-family groups claim to be a great problem. It is worth recalling that a majority of Americans see the general state of the family in the United States as declining. Americans do not seem to think that very many of their general impressions apply to them personally.

- Religion, as numerous surveys demonstrate, remains the most important common factor in the lives of Americans. Clearly Americans do not share the same religious commitments in any established church, but membership is higher in the multiple-religion groups on the whole than in any other organizations. Contributions to religious causes are higher than to any other category.[5] Nearly 90 percent of Americans say their religious beliefs are very or fairly important to them. Over 80 percent say they have a personal relationship with God. Americans pray frequently and report high attendance at religious services. *The public does not widely share the view that religion is being denied to them or forced out of public life.* Yet even this widely shared religiosity does not seem to bind Americans to common commitments beyond the expectation of personal freedom and practice in religion.

- In general, Americans see themselves as stable, whole (versus fragmented), and living lives balanced between the exciting and the routine. They also tend to pick the middle path when describing their tendencies: the majority of Americans identify themselves as being in the middle ground between traditional and progressive, spontaneous and cautious, individualistic and group-oriented. *Stability of life may be one goal that Americans hold in common.*

- In spite of the heavy emphasis in policy and in popular culture on needing therapy and various forms of victimization, very few Americans report experience of these problems. Only around 19 percent of Americans report having received counseling for a personal problem. Overwhelmingly, Americans report that they have *not* been victims of various forms of abuse: child abuse (93 percent), spousal abuse (93 percent), sexual abuse (95 percent), or other abuse (92 percent). Ninety percent of Americans say they have not been victims of sexual harassment, and the same number say they have not been victims of religious discrimination. Slightly higher numbers of Americans report they have been victims of other forms of discrimination: racial (about

17 percent), sexual (14 percent), age (15 percent). Minority groups show dissimilar tendencies only on the question of racial discrimination, where 46 percent of African Americans and 37 percent of Hispanics report they have been discriminated against. *Generally speaking, however, a "therapeutic" public policy—governmental action to solve personal problems—would receive little support.*

- Strong similarities are to be found across racial, gender, age, regional, and income lines on all of these questions (with the exception of racial discrimination). The most distinct differences appear among those with high levels of education and those who identify themselves as religious conservatives. This observation both indicates the power of these trends and points to the fact that certain concepts can still transcend traditional categories and hold common sway.

- A special note on youth: the rising generations, while not drastically different from others, are still somewhat more skeptical about government and other institutions, less religious, more relativistic, and more accepting of alternative lifestyles. Will this remain true as they age? Will public culture in the coming years be even more ungrounded and less committed to "traditional values"? It can be said that the younger age groups, while having tendencies similar to the other groups, show the highest levels of skepticism, relativism, and disaffection. If this tendency persists, then the questions raised about the future legitimacy of the American system and the need for a strong formative work become even more pronounced. The prophecies of those who predict impending crisis may prove true, even if it is not imminent.

A Changing, Pluralistic, Ambivalent Culture

This chapter has explored some general characteristics of the American people, as depicted in survey analyses, in search of some underlying common framework out of which evaluations of national life are made. The primary results show that Americans are reluctant to hold firmly to absolute norms or community interests, all the while paying service to them "in principle." Seventy-five percent of Americans agree that "we would all be better off if we could live by the same moral guidelines," but on the whole,

Americans are unable to find those common guidelines. As so many have noted, Americans are shown to be highly pragmatic when it comes to public life. Their most commonly held characteristics are high levels of personal satisfaction with job, family, local community; strong general religiosity without being specifically dogmatic; belief in the authority of the Bible; a strong sense of general public obligations; a gap between those obligations and the actual practice of them; low levels of participation in groups other than religious groups; and commitment to political reforms such as term limits, balancing the federal budget, and reducing the size of government. Do these form a sufficient base for the establishment of common life in the United States?

These qualities form some common base, but a thin one. The minimal commonality and high moral diversity of the American people actually points to a changing and realigning public culture, one which calls for a new way of describing the political landscape. A cultural reconfiguration of the American people is necessary to explain the shape of public life more thoroughly than the depictions that ideological categories or party labels now provide. Yet the unsettled ground revealed at the beginning of the twenty-first century, not least in the 2000 elections, defies general categorizations.

The greatest challenge to today's political leaders is to find a way to engage in public discourse so that the culturally divided American people can craft a means of engagement that allows consensus to emerge on the viability and sustainability of American democracy. How long can this situation of deep disaffection, triggered by the lack of moral identification with leaders, last before serious problems erupt? Is there any way to find a purpose and means of discourse to hold all this together? Many groups are seeking to advance such purposes, but none have yet succeeded in fulfilling those hopes. The difficulty of the work to be done in any formative, or preformative, project becomes even more clear as Christians continue to face their responsibilities to season, purify, reform, and perhaps lead in this new age of public challenge.

Part 2

Public Life and the Church
in the Twenty-First Century

Not only do the Americans practice their religion out of self-interest, but they often even place in this world the interest which they have in practicing it. Priests in the Middle Ages spoke of nothing but the other life; they hardly took any trouble to prove that a sincere Christian might be happy here below.

But preachers in America are continually coming down to earth. Indeed they find it difficult to take their eyes off it. The better to touch their hearers, they are forever pointing out how religious beliefs favor freedom and public order, and it is often difficult to be sure when listening to them whether the main object of religion is to procure eternal felicity in the next world or prosperity in this.

Alexis de Tocqueville, *Democracy in America*

5

Christian Public Philosophy and Theology at the Beginning of the Twenty-First Century

Elements of Formation

The church in the United States, in all its diversity and manifestations, faces a contradictory, challenging, and changing public culture. The previous chapters have attempted to describe the prevailing public culture in light of measurable attitudes and tendencies, as well as through the depiction of the varying moral-cultural constellations to be found in the United States. The church faces this public scene armed not only with its traditions and doctrines, which as in all ages seem alien and even contradictory to much of public life, but also with its own resources for the interpretation of public life and for consequent guidance on action within public realms, in the forms of public theology and Christian public philosophy. But the prevailing public culture is not only the setting for current Christian public reflection; it also shapes and influences these reflections as the church seeks to interpret the demands of Christian calling within public culture.

This chapter offers a summary look at the kinds of public inquiry being undertaken in some quarters of the church at the beginning of the new century and relates them to the picture of public culture previously laid out. These writings and activities point to sources of guidance for facing the public culture of the day, as leaders teach and prepare those in their charge, and as Christians face their public responsibilities and even hope to influence the surrounding culture. These sources are as varied as the church itself, and the conclusions they draw are likewise diverse. Yet the entire endeavor is marked by some common concerns and by characteristics that signal the unfolding Christian approach to public culture in the new millennium. The polarities or disagreements in certain categories also point to alternative approaches to be considered. As this book is intended to offer resources rather than prescriptions, this analysis keeps evaluations to a minimum, though they surely appear to some degree. But I have no hesitation about encouraging the overall endeavor of Christian public inquiry, because it demands that public life must be built on the solid ground of eternity, and not on shifting cycles or temporal commitments.

The Search for a Comprehensive Philosophy and Theology

Even in this relativistic age, the dominant tendency still found among American Christian leaders and thinkers is the desire to chart out a sustainable and comprehensive philosophy and theology of public life, as their spiritual ancestors did. In facing public life, many thinking Christians respond according to a framework made both from their obligations to particular traditions (for example, the Protestant demand for biblical sanction and authority and the Catholic demand for universal dogmatic coherence) and from the need for some central, unifying theme that offers explanations and directions for public life (such as care for the poor or for the environment as the primary test of policy, the central role of the family in building culture, or the "cultural mandate" of Genesis 1:28 establishing earthly endeavors as in the will of God). This tendency follows from the commitment to authoritative formation, and from the recognition that central ideas are necessary to a healthy society. It also demonstrates a desire for wholeness and completeness in the midst of a fragmentary culture, mimicking our eternal longings and expectations.

A related tendency found in all branches of the church, especially in evangelicalism, is the urge to hold "authoritative" gatherings that issue comprehensive manifestos or coordinated action plans and chart out direction for public issues. Recent examples from across the ecclesiastical spectrum include the Evangelical Environmental Declaration of 1991; the 1993 Chicago Declaration II; the Oxford Declarations on Faith and Economics; the Justice, Peace, and Integrity of Creation framework of the World Council of Churches; and the Pastoral Letters of the U.S. Catholic Bishops Conference on economic life and national security. These join the long line of papal encyclicals, especially those of John Paul II, in the effort to create a "magisterium" of reference for public life. Each are attempts to spell out principles drawn from underlying public theologies and philosophies and turn them into active influences on public life. Some have resulted in tangible plans of action or in organizations devoted to particular causes.

A smaller (but growing in influence) number of Christian public thinkers accept fully the difficulty, even impossibility, of developing a comprehensive guiding framework and embrace this opportunity of indeterminacy with the possibilities of creative pragmatism. "Do we even need a comprehensive public philosophy?" they ask.[1] Any public challenge or crisis is an opportunity for the church to shine if its own communal life is vigorous and healthy. Historical reflection on Christian practice gives significant guidance. The church does not need to be weighed down with strict guidelines or cumbersome philosophical declarations. As shown earlier in the work of John Milbank, this approach is typically a "principled pragmatism" (if one can accept the contradiction in terms), because it assumes that truth takes shape in practice more than in dogmatic statements and that the lives of those in the church are animated and lived out in ways that are informative and influential for the larger culture. Advocates of this approach, such as Stanley Hauerwas and John Milbank, are less concerned with defining policy or spelling out moral systems than with a fluid and dynamic interaction between church and culture. This interaction makes the church naturally political as it encounters structures of power and shapes culture by its life.

One example of the first, dominant tendency, is represented in the vision put forth in documents introducing a gathering of evangelical leaders (held in Washington, D.C. in early 1997) to discuss the state of Christian involvement in public life.

Times have obviously changed. The broadly Christian (later Judeo-Christian) cultural consensus which existed from the time of the founding until earlier in this century has been deeply eroded. With the rise of secularism and the expansion of ethnic and religious diversity, evangelicals must now make the argument for the moral principles on which the American order rests to a more diverse, less religious culture.

Evangelicals have had great difficulty in making this argument, largely because we have lacked the theological and philosophical underpinnings necessary to engage a diverse and increasingly secular culture effectively. The absence of a coherent theology of citizenship and cultural engagement among evangelicals has resulted in the use of language which creates in the public mind a suspicion that evangelicals are "intolerant" and harbor theocratic designs. . . .

Given the present opportunity for evangelical leadership in the effort to renew American culture, it is necessary to address the absence of an evangelical public theology in a concentrated manner. The proposed conference would do this by focusing on a number of critical issues. . . . At this point, we are thinking of a one or two day summit which would combine substantive input from evangelical scholars on the issues listed above, with deliberation over the content of an evangelical public theology. The immediate goal of the conference would be to issue a declaration setting forth a biblical vision of Christian citizenship and addressing the evangelical role in the renewal of American public philosophy. This declaration would be drafted in advance, finalized at the summit, and then released to the nation. . . .

This work is critical, because only a fully developed biblical understanding of the Christian role in culture and politics will enable Christians to remain committed to the patient, sustained involvement our present situation requires. Without this understanding, it will only be a matter of time before the difficulties of such involvement will lead many Christians to withdraw from the culture and return to the temporal indifference of an earlier generation. Apart from the foundation provided by an orthodox public theology, the impulse to revert back to a "separationist" mentality will be difficult to resist.[2]

Other more systematic sources of this approach include the extensive works of a multitude of Christian public philosophers and public theologians. These works include those by contemporary thinkers such as James Skillen, Paul Marshall, Richard Mouw, Nicholas Wolterstorff, Mark Noll, Jim Wallis, Max Stackhouse, Oliver O'Donovan, Joan O'Donovan, Richard John Neuhaus, George Weigel, Michael Novak, and the encyclicals and books of John Paul II. Works from earlier in the twentieth century that are still influential include those of Reinhold Niebuhr, Jacques Ellul, John Courtenay Murray, Jacques Maritain, George Grant, and Paul Ramsey. These works should be studied by leaders who want to offer direction to Christians who are challenged by their role in the formative project of building a coherent public culture.

These comprehensive works seek the goals articulated by James Skillen in a recent book:

> We believe that every citizen should engage in critical, self-conscious reflection on the deepest presuppositions about reality that control his or her approach to public life. Christians in particular, we believe, should not be so willing to accommodate themselves to . . . Enlightenment-influenced points of view. . . . They should seek to develop a coherent and comprehensive vision of God's creation order in which human society is differentiating historically and in which the political order ought to be understood.[3]

Those of an opposing tendency, however, eschew systematic definitions and range from those motivated by specific interests to those who believe that comprehensive political theology is at best contingent and at worst ideological idolatry. As the kingdom of Christ is not of this world, our relationship to it is very tenuous. Our calling is not to build civilization but to protect and build the church and to fight the forces of darkness wherever they are manifest. Interaction with culture is dynamically both critical and engaging, depending upon the demands of the times. According to Barry Harvey,

> The community of the servant-messiah is called by God to be the bearer of habits and relations which defies [sic] the present darkness—a darkness which also goes by such names as "individualism, anthropocentrism, patriarchy, mechanization, economism, consumerism, Eurocentrism, militarism, and nationalism"—by dealing with it in the context of a promised but as yet unfulfilled future, thereby giving shape and direction, sense and coherence, to the everyday practice of life. In the church, the corporate dimension of the pax Christi, God's eschatological rule is exhibited as a historical possibility and actuality.[4]

Ashley Woodiwiss refers us to other writers when he points to a new "theological turn" that has produced an increasingly ecclesiocentric argument that grounds Christian life and practice in the community of the local church. Most familiar of these theologians . . . would be Stanley Hauerwas, whose work might be considered what happens when Wendell Berry meets the Pope. Hauerwas argues theologically (and ethically) what NIMBY [not in my back yard] activists argue politically and communitiarians contend philosophically: cast your eyes away from the nation-state and efforts to prop it up . . . and go local. Hauerwas shifts our political allegiance from Christian America to the church as the community of character able to withstand the subtle power-talk of the nation-state. . . . [A] convergence among academics, community activists, and church leaders ought also to catch our attention. We might want to call this a political convergence. And its banner: "The preferential option for the local."5

Such a focus on the church means not disengagement, according to these thinkers, but "opportunities for responding to the world which are neither *strategic* nor *sectarian,* but *sacramental.*"6 In being true to its calling and by living out a holy life, the church does not define the public realm but serves it with what it really needs. "The Church, like its Jewish forbears, must learn how to cultivate the requisite skills and relations to create and maintain the kind of 'holy insecurity' that sustains a *diaspora existence,* with its nuanced interplay between participation and nonconformity, simultaneously seeking the welfare of the city wherein God has placed it while acknowledging its status as aliens within that city."7 The church must embrace its minority and pilgrim status and live out its life accordingly, faithfully practicing its characteristic virtues without seeking any predesigned strategic outcomes. In this way, the church helps shape public life though it has no grand plan for it.

The Question of Focus: Culture or Policy?

The message of the significance of culture as a focus of analysis and activism has not been lost on Christians concerned with public life. In fact, in the 1990s a debate arose among Christians over the relative importance of the emphasis on culture versus an emphasis on political action and public policy. Some writers, disillusioned with the efforts of Christians to influence politics, or embarrassed by the excesses of activist groups both left and right, advocated an exclusive emphasis on the character- and morality-formative institutions of society, such as the family, the media, and the schools. The lessons of the late 1980s from Eastern Europe, where the power of oppressive states and ideologies were defeated more by vigorous developments in religion and civil society than by direct political actions, have been instructive to Christians in the United States concerned for public life. Some thinkers have become convinced that their major concern should be to shore up the moral underpinnings of democratic society rather than to articulate a specific political agenda.

Don Eberly writes:

> Cultural recovery will only begin when evangelicals recruit and train individuals to do serious work within culture-shaping institutions themselves. While Christian political activists can frequently be heard bragging about the percentage of the electorate they represent in order to win concessions in the arena of power, the inventory of well-positioned evangelicals in publishing houses, film or entertainment, secular academia, or any number of prominent elite professions is paltry. Many of the most consequential decisions in our large and complex society are no longer made in the corridors of legislative power.[8]

Yet efforts have not ceased to spell out a clear political philosophy; if anything, the efforts of some Christians to influence legislation and elections, or to gain political office, have increased with the ascendancy of the Christian Coalition and other organized groups. The argument turns in part on the previous issue: whether it is possible to have a coherent Christian political framework—a positive vision for government, in other words—or whether politics is essentially derivative, an instrument of deeper cultural patterns. In the latter argument, political action and policy can be left to follow in the train of values and demands established elsewhere. In the first case, of course, policy—be it in the form of Supreme Court decisions, budget appropriations, or treaties—is consequential and has profound effect on the broader culture as well as on individuals.

There are many who would argue, therefore, that shaping of laws and processes is a priority demand upon those committed to Christian truth and morality. For example, Robert Dugan, head of the Washington office of the National Association of Evangelicals during the "gays in the military" controversy of the early days of the Clinton administration, wrote:

"Millions of Americans must be willing to say that homosexual activity is morally wrong, and to argue that our laws, military as well as civil, have their source in the moral law of God and the natural law foundational to our society and to all creation."[9] This is not the same as saying, with activist Tim LaHaye, "the only way to have a genuine spiritual revival is to have legislative reform,"[10] but it is to argue the place of the political realm in human order and to call it to accountability before God. Others, of course, might say that the only way to have genuine legislative reform is first to have sweeping spiritual revival, that moral reform precedes political change.

The argument over the relationship between culture and policy is rarely put in such clear alternative terms and is usually explained in terms of relative interplay between the two. Some Christian writers want to lower expectations about the extent to which faith can have bearing on political life, emphasizing the moral-cultural and personal effects. Doug Bandow has argued that "Christ's teachings emphasized the conversion of individual lives, not the reform of public institutions. Though genuine spiritual repentance has potentially far-reaching implications for how people relate in the civic sphere, that effect is only secondary."[11] On the other hand, others acknowledge the significance of the moral and cultural dimensions but insist that political effects are mandated as well: "The struggle to reshape the meaning of politics is one we must all engage in. . . . Indeed, our personal habits of political acquiescence have been central to our problems. The search for a more ethically rooted politics . . . is a journey we must make together," demands Religious Left activist Jim Wallis in *The Soul of Politics.*[12]

In his reading of sound Christian teaching on public life, the seminal and widely cited *Naked Public Square,* Richard John Neuhaus tries to solve this dilemma of emphasis, arguing for the importance of sound politics, but as an effect of sounder culture formation. "The force of virtue was thought to be both prior to and reinforcing of the polity. The polity presupposed a culture of virtue; it was not intended to replace it and could not create a new one in its place."[13] Catholic political thinker and ethicist George Weigel sums up the renewed awareness of the cultural dimensions within the public sphere experienced by many, in describing his debt to the work of John Paul II:

> The Pope's post-1989 stress on culture—better, on the revitalization of moral culture as the key to democratic renewal—has also had a marked influence on my thinking and writing. To put it simply, I am less interested in poli-

tics, the quest for power and the administrative and legislative exercise of power, than I used to be. Conversely, I find myself far more interested in the "software" side of the democratic experiment: the pre-political institutions and the habits of the mind and heart that make democracy possible. In this I am hardly alone, of course, and no doubt the current condition of American democracy has tempered my interest in the political game (narrowly construed) and helped to push my thinking down this moral-cultural path.[14]

In contrast, evangelical political philosopher Paul Marshall argues not for the superiority or inferiority of politics to culture but for a carefully differentiated perspective of the place and role of all social institutions.

> For Christians, politics cannot be the centre of existence. The Bible stresses the importance of the individual, the family, and the church, as well as government. Government is not the final authority in society; it is one institution alongside of others. . . . Yet at the same time, government is charged with the responsibility for maintaining an overall order of justice. . . . Government is not to supplant other authorities but it is to make sure that relations, such as those between person and person, between family and family, between church and church or church and state, are ones which conform to God's requirements for a just order."[15]

The discussion of these emphases and concepts points to one clear trend: the expanding awareness in the church of the breadth of public culture. Public culture cannot be reduced to politics, nor can withdrawal from the realms of political power into relatively "safe" realms of family and school be justified by doctrine or experience. Further, the old dilemma of the true relationship between evangelism on the one hand and social action on the other, which troubled generations of Christians, seems to have faded into the background as cultural and political engagement has exploded. Yet the general consensus seems to be that the church does not yet adequately engage the culture, lacking both the vision and resources for effective influence; also, the church seems not to be fully prepared for a role in political influence or power. However, at the end of the 1990s, Christian activism on both fronts of policy and culture formation was expanding rapidly to meet these challenges. The effects of these projects remain to be measured as we continue to monitor the changing shape of public culture as well as the development of Christian engagement in many spheres of human society.

Measuring the direct effects of the church on culture remains much more elusive, however, than pointing to specific legislative victories or the election of Christian officeholders.

The Special Place of the Poor and the Victimized

Christian public thinking in the late twentieth century typically contained a special theme: the place of the poor and the victimized in all social and policy considerations. For some, this is the central, unifying theme guiding Christian engagement. The identity of victims differs according to the particular concerns of advocates, but the rise of claims and theories of victimization (contrasted with demands for responsibility or acceptance of suffering) is notable. These concerns include demands for some level of resistance or struggle against oppressive forces, and they offer alternative visions of right order that will eliminate these situations.

The place of the economically poor in Christian public thought has been well-established in theological reflection. Some forms of liberation theology have interpreted Scripture and doctrine to claim that the message of the gospel is primarily to the poor and that the work of the church is primarily to be the organization of the poor against structural oppression. Oliver O'Donovan gives much credit to the work of liberation theologians for their role in the recovery of public theology, while departing from their analysis and prescription.[16] Bringing concern for the poor out of the limited realm of private charity to that of public responsibility and calling attention to institutional patterns are certainly two effects of liberation theology on the church. Responsibility to the poor is hardly questioned, even in the most conservative theological camps, at the beginning of the twenty-first century, while great differences exist on the ways in which theology informs efforts to serve them (charity, job training, public welfare, cultivation of virtue, evangelism, community organization, and so on).[17] At the beginning of his presidency in 2001, President George W. Bush introduced as one of his first initiatives a plan to allow for greater cooperation between government and "faith-based organizations" in providing such services, including making federal funds available to these organizations, and established a White House office to coordinate the necessary legislation and liaison with religious organizations. This initiative brought to fruition some policy proposals that had been advanced over many years by organizations such as the Center for Public Justice and was the result of studies funded by the Pew Charitable Trusts, among others.

But other "victims" have emerged in the consciousness of the church, and the use of this motif, as well as the particular causes taken up, demonstrate in part the extent to which the church is driven in its public life by agendas arising outside of it. If public theology is shaped by response to the real experiences of people and communities, as some hold, then Christian thinking will be directed by those experiences. In some quarters, feminist theology and "gay" theology have emerged to emphasize the centrality of liberation from oppressive norms and practices for these groups, in ways similar to the "justice" advocated for the poor by liberation theologians. In recent years, some activists also have made nonhuman species and the environment central to their theology, complete with a critique of exploitive human practices and a call for the liberation of the environment from its oppressors.

More conservative Christian groups have also developed this theme, as Christians themselves take the role of victims of secular society. Cries are heard that children in public schools are forced to imbibe heresy and are refused their rights of religious practice, and that Christian groups are denied access to public spaces for religious purposes. Internationally, the cause of persecuted Christians has led some advocates to employ analogies of the Holocaust, claiming that Christians now take the role formerly held by the Jews in receiving the wrath of persecuting governments and non-Christian religious leaders. Religious persecution at home and abroad has perhaps become the major policy focus of activist Christian organizations. Christian activism in the 1990s included the coordinated effort to pass the Religious Freedom Restoration Act in 1993 and the concentration on international religious persecution in such endeavors as opposition to the renewal of the Most Favored Nation trade status of China.

Ralph Reed Jr., former director of the Christian Coalition, states that

religious conservatives have not brought all their problems on themselves. Equally to blame are the media, which inadequately cover the positive and affirming side of religious faith, and tend to report only activities and statements that reinforce a negative stereotype. A prime example was the infamous description of evangelicals by Michael Weisskopf in a front-page story in the Washington Post: "poor, uneducated, and easy to command." . . .

When Martin Luther King, Jr. . . . . proclaimed that "just law is a man-made
code that squares with the moral law or the law of God," no one objected
to his introduction of religion into a public-policy issue. But similar refer-
ences to God's law made by conservative religious leaders in connection with
such causes as opposition to abortion are likely to elicit hysterical cries that
they threaten the "separation of church and state."[18]

Of course, the most widely cited victims are the unborn, whose cause
has been central to much of Christian activism for decades. Quite often the
argument made against abortion has less to do with the immorality of the
act of abortion or the character of those causing the abortion than with
the rights of the unborn and the violation of those rights by mothers, doc-
tors, and the state. Unborn children are the ultimate helpless victims, anal-
ogous to the innocent victims of invasion whose defense is justified under
the terms of just-war theory. Those who use violence against clinics base
their actions on the principle of justifiable forcible intervention to save the
lives of the helpless.

Surveys consulted in this study indicated a strong sense of suspicion
among self-identified Christians toward cultural leaders and institutions,
perhaps because of agreement with analyses like Reed's. On questions regarding whether the nation is in decline or improving, evangelicals and traditional Catholics showed very strong perceptions of decline in education,
the media, the arts, and other nonpolitical sectors. They were also among
groups showing the strongest suspicion of leadership, lack of trust in the
competence of government, and concern about other institutions, particularly the schools and the media. They agreed in large numbers with the
view that national elites do not uphold Christian values and beliefs. The
general sense of being under attack is very strong among religious Americans, as is the idea that their beliefs are now insignificant to public life.

However, when asked if they personally had been victims of religious
discrimination, only 9 percent of evangelicals and 8 percent of conservative Catholics indicated they had been. This compares with 12 percent of
secularists who claimed experiences of religious discrimination and 10 percent of the American people as a whole.

So why do these groups express such strong perceptions of hostility? Is
this another example of the inconsistencies to be found in survey results?
It is more likely that the development of this concern is another result of
the emergence of the theme of culture in Christian public analysis. As a cul-

tural agenda is advanced, consciousness of the hostility of the surrounding culture also increases, even though specific instances of hostility are hard to find. Culture reforming and culture shaping go hand in hand with protection from culture. All of these movements are aspects of the important adjustment now under way in the church to the reality that the United States, and the West in general, is now pluralistic and "post-Christian," as many have termed it. The victimology is perhaps overdone, but it is symptomatic of the strong sense of decline, suspicion, and even fear shown in survey responses and in the general awareness of the surrounding culture. Increasing cultural pluralism and declining Christian consensus are widely perceived. These concerns are strongly evident among evangelicals and traditional Catholics, who are the largest and fastest growing groups of American Christians. The most famous examples of this perception are the proclamation in 1999 by conservative Christian leader Paul Weyrich that Christians had "lost the culture wars" and should forget about political agendas and concentrate on building their own cultural institutions, and the surprising book by Cal Thomas and Ed Dobson, *Blinded by Might: Can the Religious Right Save America?* in which the authors challenge the temptation of power and call for the church to give up political action.[19]

The Form of Public Authority: Theocracy or Democracy

In part because of the growing awareness of religious freedom problems both inside and outside the United States, Christian public reflection is also concerned at the beginning of the twenty-first century with the question of what political structures and processes are legitimate. The major question is whether the church should support and encourage democracy. Can Christians still give general support to the prevailing American concepts of freedom and representative government, or must these now give way?

Since the setting of the biblical narratives is in the context of empires and monarchies, and any direct biblical political instructions are addressed to rulers and subjects in that context, it could be argued that we must choose either to adopt an insistence on antiquated structure or to assume the irrelevance of Scripture and tradition to contemporary public life with its democratic tendencies. More practically, the chaos, secularity, and even immorality of modern politics leads many Christians to wonder if some sort of theocracy or established form of the accountability of politics to religion would not be preferable to contemporary pluralism. Perhaps it would be better just to start over with a better system. Biblical passages make a *prima facie* case for strong temporal authority and submission to it—for example, Paul's injunctions to obey secular rulers and to recognize their legitimate role in keeping social order (Rom. 13:1–7). On the other hand, twentieth-century experience, as well as the record of history, demonstrates that strong temporal power is often cruel, proud, and oppressive. Such regimes typically attempt to eliminate spiritual authority as a rival for power and usually cause great suffering for Christians and others.

These contemporary experiences lead many Christians who wrestle with the question of how modern democracy in any form can be justified and supported. Since no definite examples of democratic politics can be found in the Bible, nor really in much of the experience of the church, Christian arguments for democracy are built on general principles and historical arguments. Throughout its history, much of the political thinking within the church concentrated on the duties of monarchs and their obligations to God and the church. In the modern age, concepts derived from Scripture and tradition, such as creational human dignity (as a source of rights and a requirement for consent to be governed), the delegated and limited authority of earthly leaders, the accountability of leaders to transcendent law, and historical differentiation under the progress of redemption, among others, have been used to find support for democracy. Yet the question of the legitimacy of democracy continues to be raised, not least because modern democracy seems to be built on secular and self-oriented foundations, and in this age of postmodern suspicion of these premises, the challenges run deep. Further, the unending sinfulness and cruelty of human beings leads one to wonder if democracy really is preferable, or ever sustainable, since freedom so often gives opportunity for disorder and exploitation.

Would not a more stable, hierarchical, fixed-expectation community be preferable and more biblical? Should we not abandon the notions of equality and complete freedom of opportunity in favor of communities that are stable and "organic," that is, well-coordinated, interrelated, and devoted to noble human ends? Can we not accept that some have been given the right to rule by virtue of their abilities and preparation, and that the rest of us have other callings? Should we not establish mechanisms to uphold the authority of higher law because it comes from ultimate sources, even if it is inconvenient and we would rather not give it our consent? Such a communitarian ideal has been encouraged in recent years by thinkers who assess modern liberal democracy as flawed and ultimately destructive of human good because it places unlimited and ever-expanding rights above the true good. For example, Canadian political philosopher George Parkin Grant argues, in reference to modern permissiveness toward abortion, that rights and freedom must be understood in the larger framework of truth, not as self-defined entitlements.

> The legal and political system, which was the noblest achievement of the English-speaking societies, came forth from our long tradition of free institutions and Common Law, which was itself produced and sustained by centuries of Christian belief. Ruthlessness in law and politics was limited by a system of legal and political rights which guarded the individual from the abuses of arbitrary power, both by the state and other individuals. The building of this system has depended on the struggle and courage of many, and was fundamentally founded on the Biblical assumption that human beings are the children of God. For this reason, everybody should be properly protected by carefully defined rights. Those who advocate easy abortion in the name of rights are at the same time unwittingly undermining the very basis of rights. Their complete disregard for the rights of the unborn weakens the very idea of rights itself. . . . A technological vision of man or woman as an object means that we can apply our "improvements" to them as objects with increasing efficiency. Once we deny justice to any human life, then we are well on the road to the kind of thinking that impels a fascist dictatorship to the horrors of the death camp and the purge.[20]

Because of the perceived flaws in modern concepts of democracy, many Christian thinkers have sought to articulate a distinct, carefully defined approach to democracy that places power in the service of human needs and the ultimate good. Oliver O'Donovan asserts that "political institutions are . . . too fluid to assume an ideal form, since they are the work of Providence in the changing affairs of successive generations." Therefore, it is not the function of political theology "to describe an ideal set of political institutions."[21] One can say that in certain circumstances monarchy or oligarchy may be preferable if they are organized for the common good and limited by traditions or by other checks on their power. Further, the changing shape of political institutions suggests that historical forms may yield to others unknown, under the impact of globalization or international mass movements or religious revivals.

Nonetheless, according to O'Donovan, "a Christian theologian can venture to characterize a *normative political culture* broadly in continuity with the Western liberal tradition."[22] This claim resonates with the beliefs of many other Christians. O'Donovan finds the Western liberal tradition to be properly the heir of Christendom, through its adoption of the concepts of limited government *under law* and of responsible government for the common good, embodied in constitutionalism. Specific forms of democracy (presidential, parliamentary, federal, mixed, and so on) can vary according to situation and need, but the overall principles can be supported. The problem in this late modern period, which O'Donovan recognizes, is that Western liberal society has left these moorings in pursuit of absolute freedom for the "unencumbered self" and has lost the transcendent grounding for responsible and limited government. Its sustainability therefore is uncertain, even though the world rushed to embrace Western democracy in the upheavals of the 1980s and 1990s. It may yet collapse upon itself as expectations grow and demands increase.

Tentative affirmation of democracy is a common thread in the church. C. S. Lewis believed that "if we had not fallen . . . patriarchal monarchy would be the sole lawful government. But since we have learned sin, we have found . . . that 'all power corrupts, and absolute power corrupts absolutely.'"

> I believe in political equality. But there are two opposite reasons for being a democrat. You may think all men so good that they deserve a share in the government of the commonwealth, and so wise that the commonwealth needs their advice. That is, in my opinion, the false, romantic doctrine of democracy. On the other hand, you may believe fallen men to be so wicked that not one of them can be trusted with any irresponsible power over his fellows. That I believe to be the true ground of democracy.[23]

Lewis's negative ground for democracy is moderated somewhat by Reinhold Niebuhr's famous 1944 dictum: "Man's capacity for justice makes democracy possible; but man's inclination to injustice makes democracy necessary." His tentative yet affirmative stance, expressed at the opening of the postwar age, still characterizes well the efforts to apply Christian insights to political structures. Christian advocates of democracy on the whole have not been sentimental or sanguine about human moral capabilities; they agree with Niebuhr that "modern democracy requires a more realistic philosophical and religious basis [than rationalism], not only in order to anticipate and understand the perils to which it is exposed; but also to give it a more persuasive justification."[24] A Christian-shaped culture provides such a basis, according to Niebuhr, since it is clearheaded about human propensities.

As the church begins its life in the twenty-first century, it can consult an abundance of reflections by Christians on the question of support for democracy. Most contemporary Christian public thinkers demonstrate a preference for some form of democracy, though some raise questions about an absolute commitment to it. Many see serious warning signs about the sustainability of democracy. Some of the most persuasive prodemocratic advocacy comes from American Roman Catholics, such as George Weigel, Richard John Neuhaus, and Michael Novak. Other advocates include the neo-Calvinists, arguing from a "common grace" tradition, for whom the moral law is embedded in creation and accessible to all, thereby allowing for a degree of self-government.

George Weigel's systematic work on the basis for democracy is illustrative. He refers to principles drawn from the writings of theologian John Courtenay Murray in laying out five "foundational truths" for the support of American democracy. These formulate a good summary of the arguments for late twentieth century Christian commitment to democratic governance.

1. "God is sovereign over nations as well as individuals," meaning no government can claim absolute power, an idea which "sets limits on the boundaries of the political, even as it invests politics with its own proper dignity."
2. "The human person has the God-given capacity to be self-governing," which is demonstrated in the freedom given to persons to obey, to choose, and to be judged for their actions.
3. "Just governance—governance that is congruent with the dignity of human beings as persons, as moral agents—is by, through, and with the consent of the governed."
4. "There is a sense of justice inherent in the people by which they are empowered to judge, direct, and correct the processes of government," which is not given by the governors but comes from other sources in "civil society" and from created human nature.

5. "Only a virtuous people can be free. . . . free government in a free society is not inevitable, only possible, and . . . its possibility can be realized publicly only when the people are governed inwardly by the "universal moral law," a principle that qualifies the demand for democracy according to cultural capacities.[25]

Such principles, while not in any way assuming the universal possibility of or expectation for democracy, are intended to give Christians an anchor of preference for democracy and an agenda for advocacy of and participation in democratic government in this age of political change and uncertainty. These analysts also premise the possibility of democratic governance on a culture in which virtue is widely practiced and the universal moral law is widely understood. Freedom is only possible where the people have the capacity for self-governance.

The demand for religious freedom, therefore, has been a driving force in cultivating Christian support for democracy in the United States. The American experience of nonestablishment of religion, religious pluralism, and relatively low levels of governmental interference in religious life is of great benefit to churches. An open, limited public order gives the church a wider range both to pursue its mission and to differentiate into the highly diverse forms it expresses in the United States. So the demand for religious freedom has often been the lead item on the political agenda of the church in the United States. According to George Weigel, the primary demands of the church on the world are (1) the "demand for space," or freedom to pursue the church's characteristic practices of Word and sacrament, and (2) the demand that the world "consider the possibility of redemption," or that it be open to the moral and cultural possibilities that emanate from the life of the church.[26]

Skeptics of such arguments, however, are also to be found in the church. They challenge the ability of humans to realize these principles in the context of a modern, individualistic society. Democracy, in this perspective, is a false hope for Christians, because it is ultimately built on false assumptions about human beings and their capacity for virtue. Modern democracy has been and still is devoted to the destruction of godly principles and to replacing them with human autonomy and raw power. Swedish philosopher Tage Lindblom sums up this perspective:

Society is a living organism and properly should be the carrier of a hierarchy of values, of unshakable spiritual and moral norms; society is of the qualitative order. But this commonwealth is now threatened with replacement by a centralized world of bureaucracy whose aim is to dominate the vacuum that a withering civilization is leaving behind. The modern industrial and social state is quantitative in nature and, as centralized bureaucracy, it has no moral norms. . . . Once upon a time, in traditional societies, laws were complements and confirmations of an order of things that had its profoundest roots in the spiritual realm and in a social morality deriving from that realm. Now we see the opposite. . . . The scope for responsible citizenship is steadily eroded; man will become more and more a subject.[27]

Survey data illustrate well the dilemma facing the practice of democracy at the beginning of the twenty-first century. While support for democratic principles is strong, alienation from national leaders and institutions is high. While expressions of commitment to civil life are high, participation in the democratic process is low. The presidential election of 2000 was an occasion for widespread disaffection and cynicism over the possibilities of national democracy. In the eyes of many, the process is not yielding the promised results. And if self-government indeed requires both a common sense of the public good and a well-formed, virtuous citizenry, the generally low levels of consensus and moral commitment charted in earlier chapters do not bode well for democracy in America. Further, Christians struggle to accept a system that they believe could be founded on spiritual principles but which in experience seems even less devoted to those principles and ever more bent on relativism and sensualism. Hence the high levels of distrust of leaders and disaffection with the culture found in the most conservative Christians in America.

Pluralism, Differentiation, and Civil Society

In light of the dilemmas posed by the modern definition and practice of democracy and the problems associated with drawing liberal principles from Scripture, many Christian thinkers have found grounding in the concept of *principled pluralism*. This term summarizes much of the work undertaken in the 1980s and 1990s to develop Christian concepts of democracy and to provide a way to support democracy in the face of the challenges to it. Similar concepts found their way into public discourse during election campaigns, in such forms as promoting "public-private partnerships" and supporting nongovernmental institutions that provide social services. Unfortunately, this way of thinking holds little demonstrable place among the American public. While surveys demonstrated commitment to some forms of "limited government" and "natural rights" beliefs, they showed that the American people in the main still hold a simple statism as their political doctrine. The American public as a whole does not articulate a robust, differentiated public perspective.

Principled pluralism is a way of explaining and accepting the diversity to be found in public life and of spelling out the basis for Christian resistance to authoritarianism and totalitarianism, even when public chaos may seem to warrant a coherent, strong hand. In this framework, many different modes of life have both their own purposes and their own authority structures because God created a diverse and differentiated world. No single structure—political, economic, or cultural—should dominate the others. God mediates his power on earth through various offices or representatives rather than exercising it directly; his authority is never concentrated in any one person or any one earthly institution. So families have particular purposes and powers, as do economic, religious, and other institutions. Such an approach is used to validate democracy—in the sense of constitutionally limited governmental purpose and power, human rights, and citizen participation—while not taking the modern liberal route leading to individualism at the expense of community, or voluntarism at the expense of morality and law. This view also carries an understanding of historical development that allows Christians to explain how different political norms can be valid in different times and places. Catholic teachings, such as the doctrine of subsidiarity, and Protestant concepts of differentiation are similar in these conclusions. The concept of "civil society" with its "mediating structures," referring to the interaction of the various aspects and institutions of life, has become a common way to describe the pluralistic ideal and contrasts with the organic picture of society laid out by Lindblom and others.[28]

This perspective also leads to the central concern for religious freedom and the call to Christians to accept diversity even with its shortcomings. Luis Lugo summarizes this perspective in his review of Christian political philosophy:

> A Christian commitment to confessional pluralism is based neither on the pragmatic necessity of having to live in a religiously diverse society nor on a desire for an accommodation with the relativistic spirit of the age. It is based,

rather, on a principled understanding of the nature and limits of political community. The fact that pluralists see all attempts to duplicate the theocratic model as essentially misguided does not at all mean that they believe the state should govern apart from any transcendent moral norms. It means only that they believe the state should govern according to the norms appropriate to it as an institution of God's common grace.[29]

That is, with limited and well-defined roles and purposes.

Some Christian writers, perceiving the differentiation in creation, have explored the relationship between this phenomenon and the plurality of the Triune Godhead. Max Stackhouse's observation that "inherent in every human civilization is a tendency to plurality, one that requires a certain pluralism of institutional formation," enables Christians to offer "metaphysical-moral grounding for dealing with the pluralism at hand," because belief in the Triune God enables one to know that "pluralism is a normative theological belief as well as an ethical or social belief."[30]

This insight is an important correction to ideologies that call for the ultimate unity of all human associations, such as Marxism, which foresees the penultimate absorption of all things into the state, and totalitarian or theocratic religious beliefs, such as found in some forms of Islam. It is also a correction to the simple reductions to be found among some Christian public commentators and the simple statism of those who believe the government is ultimately responsible for all problems.

However, as Richard Mouw and Sander Griffioen point out in commenting on Stackhouse's "metaphysical-moral" pluralism, the observable fact of general pluralism does not automatically give sanction to any particular existing human institution. While "Christians can enthusiastically support the program of supporting associational diversity, . . . they will also insist that this endorsement must be viewed against the background of a larger account of what human flourishing is all about."[31] The variability of human practices and needs will bring about great variety in structures in different times and places, yet the larger framework of ultimate human good does not necessarily grant permanence to any existing or ideal institutional structure. Creational pluralism does not automatically justify modern democracy. Further, simply pointing to differentiation does not in and of itself provide direction to institutions as to how they should go about serving the greater good. A Christian formative project based on this approach

will have to further spell out for these institutions and for citizens the implications of such principles.

Also of consequence to the commitment to principled pluralism is the
evidence in recent surveys that the American public shows little receptiv-
ity to these concepts. The term *pluralism* means "toleration," and even "anything goes" in general usage, when it is applied to moral and policy choices.
Pluralism does not signify a sophisticated grasp of the purposes of and relationships among multiple institutions in the common parlance. Further,
the growing disappointment of the American people with national government follows from their high expectations for it and their dependence
upon it. As noted, Americans still expect the national government to be
primarily responsible for the solution of national problems—meaning that
Americans may lack a robust sense of the importance of other institutions.
The great gap between high civic-mindedness (or commitment to the public good) and the low levels of civic participation in a variety of institutions
points to a growing vacuum that could be filled by an increasingly powerful state.

To qualify this concern, it is true that surveys also show that Americans
in general are more satisfied with local and regional governments than with
the national, and more satisfied with local circumstances in contrast with
their concerns over national decline. Their actual practices may belie the
conceptual tendencies the survey data point to. More will be said about this
in the next chapter. Yet the very high commitment shown by Americans to
a few ideas of the "American Creed" (including federalism, limited national
government, civil rights, and civic responsibilities) has a static and even nostalgic quality and indicates little in the way of extensive thought by Americans about the nature of public life. Lip service is easily given to well-worn
principles.

Is it possible, then, for these elaborated Christian democratic foundations to inform and guide American democracy in the new century? Can
the formative project of political philosophy and theology, demanded by
so many to develop a healthy, differentiated society and encourage civic
responsibility, be successful in the current cultural environment? The signs
are not promising under current conditions, suggesting that much more
intensive and extensive work, perhaps even divine intervention, will be necessary for the effects sought by proponents. The signs do point, however,
to the significance of local practice as the basis for a beginning for this project, as the real life of the church and other local communities receive the

loyalty of citizens, provide experience in self-governance, and offer resistance to the encroachment of distant powers. It could be that the practical necessity of freedom for the church to be the church, and related commitments to limits on the power of the state, is a more powerful argument for pluralism than one that searches for scriptural validations of current earthly structures.

The Problem of Experiential Pluralism

No discussion of Christian approaches to public life is complete without reference to the oft-noted erosion of a Judeo-Christian consensus that is considered to have been the foundation of life in the United States. This change is widely perceived, even if historical studies and other analyses raise questions about the degree to which America actually had a Christian foundation. We have already used the term *pluralism* in reference to the principled efforts by Christian writers to provide a "metaphysical-moral" foundation for diversity in public life. For most, however, the term *pluralism* refers to the experience of moral, ethnic, cultural, and preferential diversity increasing in American life: the social facts of plurality.

Survey analyses validate in many ways the common-sense perceptions of moral pluralism in the United States, even as they show some areas of wide consensus. The various cultural clusters evident in the United States demonstrate this pluralism clearly. Census data, along with daily experiences even in small communities, reveal increasing ethnic and religious pluralism. Surveys point to a number of areas in which public culture either entertains new questions about old assumptions (life and death, family and sexuality, the basis of law, and so on) or shows growing acceptance of relaxed moral judgments, even among those of religious orientation, thus creating gaps among Americans between traditional and more "progressive" groups. The already noted increase in acceptance of homosexuality and of assisted termination of life are clear examples.

Ronald Thiemann expresses the effects experiential pluralism has on public life in his effort to find some common role for public theology in American life:

> The dizzying diversity of contemporary culture has created a climate in which many people are sorely tempted to withdraw from involvement in public

life. They recognize the profundity of our cultural differences, despair of all attempts to adjudicate those disagreements, and so, weary of the strident public debates, retreat to private enclaves of like-minded persons. Those who succumb to this temptation implicitly or explicitly deny that there can be any meaningful public life; consequently, they seek to cultivate a few precious values that might endure within homogeneous communities separated from the public world. . . . But, all versions of the strategy of withdrawal fail to do justice to the complexity of the Christian gospel. Those who despair of any meaningful public life fail to recognize the enduring presence of God's creative hand in the public realm. In so doing, they rob the world of that theological virtue most needed in American public life—the virtue of hope. . . . [They] assume that our differences are so profound that we cannot work together for some common human good.[32]

Thiemann and others hope that the church's historical experience of surviving internal pluralism may also provide a major public demonstration of meaningful interaction even when differences threaten to destroy. They believe that the fears normal to experiences of difference can be overcome by the grace normative to Christians. This forward-looking embrace of experiential pluralism is difficult for many to accept; distress and frustration are perhaps more common. But Christians are enabled to accept the reality of a more competitive, less consensual culture even if they struggle against it.

The Question of Legitimacy

Because of increasing alienation from the dominant strains of public culture, growing awareness of hostility on the part of social and cultural elites toward religion and traditional morality, and because of certain troubling developments in public policy, some Christian leaders have become willing to entertain the possibility that the government of the United States has lost legitimacy and that resistance to it is demanded. This might be expected from some quarters of the Christian Right and from some of the extreme militia groups that claim Christian authority or name themselves in biblical terms (for example, the "Army of God," who claimed credit for the bombings of Atlanta abortion clinics and gay bars in 1998). At the end of the twentieth century even some mainstream Christian leaders began to demand that the church face this question. They base their concerns on specific policies, such as legislative acts or court decisions, and on the conclusion that certain institutions have overstepped their authority and are imposing cultural permissivism on the American public.

In early 2001, many conservative Christians were distressed to see President Bush's nominee for Attorney General of the United States, Senator John Ashcroft of Missouri, subjected to hostile questioning and ridicule, largely because of his evangelical beliefs and commitments to social conservatism. During hearings on his nomination, examining senators shined a spotlight on his past legislative efforts as well as his faith and seriously raised the question of whether he would be able to enforce the "laws of the land" because of those beliefs. Leaders of activist groups raised the possibility that he would engage in witch-hunts regarding judicial nominees and would "force his religion" on the rest of the country. In contrast, during the 2000 election many mainstream groups found much to praise in Democratic vice-presidential candidate Joe Lieberman's open commitment to Orthodox Judaism and his public statements about the place of faith in public life. Many conservative Christians saw this inconsistency as a continuation of efforts to rid public life of perspectives based on Christian principles.

The best-known example of arguments for the illegitimacy of our democratic system is found in the 1996–97 discussions, carried out in the form of a symposium, in the pages of *First Things,* the leading journal of religion and culture. The title of the symposium was "The End of Democracy? The Judicial Usurpation of Politics." In his introduction to the symposium the editor of the journal, Richard John Neuhaus, laid out the case:

> This symposium addresses many similarly troubling judicial actions that add up to an entrenched pattern of government by judges that is nothing less than the usurpation of politics. The question here explored, in full awareness of its far-reaching consequences, is whether we have reached or are reaching the point where conscientious citizens can no longer giver moral assent to the existing regime. . . . The government of the United States of America no longer governs by the consent of the governed. With respect to the American people, the judiciary has in effect declared that the most important questions about how we ought to order our life together are outside the purview of "things of their knowledge."[33]

Neuhaus's concerns are expressed in specific reference to Supreme Court decisions of the mid-1990s that overturned decisions made by state legislatures or by public referenda that upheld traditional standards on homosexuality, abortion, and euthanasia. The judicial reasoning of the 1973 *Roe v. Wade* decision is also in his mind. Neuhaus further challenges these developments:

> Law, as it is presently made by the judiciary, has declared its independence
> from morality. Indeed . . . morality—especially traditional morality, and
> most especially morality associated with religion—has been declared legally
> suspect and a threat to public order. Among the most elementary principles
> of Western Civilization is the truth that laws which violate the moral law
> are null and void and must in conscience be disobeyed . . . [This] was . . .
> the principle invoked by the founders of the nation, . . . by Martin Luther
> King, Jr., . . . [and] today by, among many others, Pope John Paul II.[34]

The significance of this challenge, laid out by a leading Catholic interpreter of public life, is enormous. It summarizes the questions faced by all Christians working within a culture that is in many ways antagonistic. It also raises directly the questions many have about this particular democracy in the United States, going well beyond the discussions outlined earlier about the general bases of support for democracy and the principles of sound government spelled out by various Christians. Symposium participant Charles Colson stated: "Only the Church collectively can decide at what point a government becomes sufficiently corrupt that a believer must resist it. But, with fear and trembling, I have begun to believe that, however Christians in America gather to reach their consensus, we are fast approaching this point."[35]

These statements were not universally hailed, and years of debate over these questions lie before the church. Many dissenters to the perspectives of Colson and Neuhaus challenged the thrust of the argument; for example, William Bennett cautioned:

> We are still America, not "Amerika." This premise ought to guide our future
> deliberations. Of course this nation has suffered tremendous moral regres-
> sion during the last three decades. But the situation is not irreversible and
> our government is not illegitimate. My concern with declaring the Ameri-
> can "regime" illegitimate is that it assumes that because of the actions of an
> out-of-control Court, America has become (or is about to become) a nation

that is irredeemably antidemocratic, that we have exhausted all our options, that we are powerless to rein in the Court. That is simply not so. We have available to us the means. The question for our time is: do enough people have the will? I simply do not know the answer to that question—nor do I think enough has been done to inform citizens to be confident of the answer. We need to find out the answer to that question, and soon. Because one thing is for sure, and on this I think we can all agree: the stakes are very high indeed and the hour is late.[36]

Yet it is surprising that so many conservative Christian leaders, who represent some of the constituencies that have provided a major source of legitimacy and stability to the United States public order, are now going beyond challenging policies to questioning the very structure and basis of secular public life. The Christian Left has long been associated with questioning the legitimacy of the United States, for reasons ranging from its "capitalist exploitation" of the poor to its "imperialistic" foreign policies and its history of "racism." But the response of evangelical leader James Dobson to the questions raised indicates the level to which this debate has been raised:

I stand in a long tradition of Christians who believe that rulers may forfeit their divine mandate when they systematically contravene the divine moral law. The accumulation of evidence, when combined with the lawless jurisprudence that produced it, should remove all doubt that our judiciary has, by act and intention, stepped out from under the moral law upon which governing authority depends. They have made it plain that they have no intention of regarding any higher law than themselves and that those who do will not be tolerated in the public square. Having tortured the First Amendment to exclude all but "secular" motives from public debate, Justice Kennedy, writing for the Court, goes on to include in the definition of religious belief those who hold that "there is an ethic and a morality which transcend human invention." Therefore, whether you believe government derives its legitimacy from the consent of the governed or from a higher source, *our government has clearly transgressed its bounds in such a manner as to lose its authority* (emphasis mine). This is where we are. The pressing question is, where do we go from here?[37]

Dobson goes on to challenge Christian leaders and pastors to consider the calling to risk rejection and labels of "extremism" in order to provide a basis for the necessary reform movement that must be guided by the moral law of God. None of the writers in the forum has called for armed resistance or wholesale emigration, nor even for building conclaves in Montana, and they want to go slowly in their considerations of courses of action. Their critics accuse them of giving some legitimacy to those who do commit violence or withdraw to alternative societies. At the least, raising these issues in these forms reveals again the contingency and incompleteness of public life for those who are committed to "a far greater city."

Such questions have been faced by the church in many different ages and situations. Typically the questions are forced by tyranny: do we acknowledge the legitimacy of this emperor or dictator or party, even though we are persecuted, since God wills the existence of civil government for purposes of peace and order; or do we resist and even undermine the regime? Christians in Nazi Germany and the Soviet empire, in ancient Rome and in contemporary Sudan, Indonesia, Morocco, and Pakistan, have been forced to face these issues. But these are rare and troubling questions for a democracy, which gains its legitimacy in great part by consent, as well as by its conformity to recognized moral norms. In this case, the concerns draw attention to the deep stresses that are emerging in American public life, and to the shape of battles to come. They demonstrate the fissures within the Christian community as well, as to what our legitimate expectations for public life should be, and therefore, what the nature of the formative project might be.

The Quest for New Foundations

The problem of pluralism, coupled with civic decline and growing challenges to the legitimacy of American democracy, leads to consideration of the real possibilities for reconstituting some common basis for American culture. Increasing pluralism gives rise to perceptions of an erosion of cultural consensus, doubts about the ability of current national institutions to uphold moral and cultural standards, new questions about the legitimacy of the American experiment, and a general lack of trust. These perceptions then lead to calls for renewed commitments to some common core for civic life. Many leaders want to find some basis upon which to rebuild community in the United States.

Among those with religious commitments, this is not a new concern. Further, the faithful often suggest that the solution to cultural crisis is the rediscovery of religious foundations. Richard Weaver wrote in 1968:

> The challenge is to save the human spirit by re-creating a non-materialist society. Only this can rescue us from a future of nihilism, urged on by the demoniacal force of technology and by our own moral defeatism. The first step will be to give the common man a world view completely different from that which he has constructed out of his random knowledge of science. . . . What man thinks about the world when he is driven back to his deepest reflections and most secret promptings will finally determine all that he does. . . . The creation of a religious moral world will bring an end to the downward conversion which today threatens institutions and culture.[38]

Other Christians have called for the church to find a coherent principle for public life in the potentially unifying causes that address pressing contemporary concerns. The primary candidates put forth at the beginning of the new millennium by various liberal Christians were (1) environmental liberation and (2) globalism in all its forms. On environmentalism, Christian programs have joined those of other perspectives to suggest that our primary public responsibility is stewardship, that cultivating and caring for our common earthly home constitutes both the most pressing human crisis and the greatest opportunity for common human pursuit of the good. Calvin DeWitt asserts: "Environmental responsibility lies at the center of Christian faith and life, requiring every person who professes Christ to be faithful in their care and keeping of the creation."[39] Ian Bradley has summed up the perspective shared by many:

> I believe that Christianity . . . offers faith, hope and also a positive role to play in preserving and saving the environment. I am equally sure that if Christians fail to speak on what is almost certainly the most important issue of our time and do not enter into dialogue with those who are concerned about the environment, we will not only have lost an enormous missionary and pastoral opportunity but we will have failed the human race, the planet and, most important of all, we will have failed God; the Father who knows and cares about one sparrow falling from heaven, the Son who communed with and redeemed the wayward forces of nature and the Holy Spirit who broods over the face of the waters just as she moves within our souls.[40]

Advocates of globalism have similar concerns. The world needs new, integrated institutions to overcome the divisions of state, nation, tribe, and other forms of particularity. And the world needs a new perspective of common humanity to allow humans to cooperate in this task of global community. Canadian theologian Douglas John Hall declares that

> there are no parts any more, if by parts we mean separable entities whose destiny can be lived out in isolation from all the rest. The globe is one single and continuous whole. It will either survive as one or it will not survive. The boundaries between earth's historical parts are geographically and biospherically untenable. No border between nations, no matter how well-armed, can prevent the fall of acid rain or the fallout from nuclear accidents. From outer space, it is said, the only visible historical boundary is the Great Wall of China. . . .
>
> It is no longer mere doctrinal and biblical faithfulness that drives responsible Christians to try to make good their own message of reconciliation; the biblical injunction to global unity has become a political necessity—indeed, a matter of life and death.[41]

Some conservative Christians have advocated other themes as centralizing principles. The most familiar, associated with groups such as the Christian Coalition and the Family Research Council, seek to place preservation and protection of the family at the center of cultural and political renewal. The "Contract with the American Family" that these groups advanced during the 1996 election campaign is a good example of this agenda. The belief in the centrality of family life has also spawned movements aimed at men, such as PromiseKeepers and the National Fatherhood Initiative, and has continued solidarity with the ongoing pro-life movement.

But other Christian thinkers question whether it is necessary or even possible to find a coherent set of constitutive principles for public life. Perhaps the simple practices of community, with well-established procedures and patterns, provide ample scope for a community to function, with no declarations or myths required. Pluralism, in any case, mitigates against such foundations, according to these thinkers, and attempts to establish religious foundations will fail or lead to cruelty and repression. Interaction between diverse religious groups and their faithfulness to acting in love will have a dynamic impact. According to Ronald Thiemann, "religious pluralism can be an important resource in the search for a new common good for America. . . .

The real challenge to a North American public theology is to find a way—within the social, cultural, and religious pluralism of North American politics—to influence the development of public policy without seeking to construct a new Christendom or lapsing into a benign moral relativism."[42]

This argument brings us back to one of the original questions, exemplified in the conversations within the arenas of public philosophy and public theology. Christian leaders must decide whether to devote time and effort to the formative project, whether to teach and lead and organize to establish a sound foundational framework in public life. The questions raised about legitimacy by other Christian leaders also force us to face up to the kind of discussions that may be necessary. Unfortunately, surveys and other sources of information indicate the difficulty of such an undertaking. Christians themselves vary greatly with each other in their concepts of public life. No clear and widely accepted systematic approach is discernible, other than a few very general affirmations. Because of this, any Christian strategy for the reconstruction of public culture currently has little chance of wide acceptance. The practice of faithfulness may indeed be the best goal, since in community any commonality that might exist among Christians will be seen.

For example, the increasing disaffection with public life, as seen in widespread rejection of secular public education, and the consequent practical adjustments by churches—founding their own schools and cultivating homeschooling—may point to an existing, effectually operating pluralistic public philosophy that demands differentiation. The acting out of principle is far more effective than any comprehensive declaration could be.

Christians are increasing their demands that the tenets of the moral law as defined in religious traditions—even when these tenets differ from the findings of secular, scientific rationalism—be considered in major public decisions. By holding firmly to a biblical concept of life rather than the one derived from science and by working both quietly and publicly to save life—unborn and suffering—Christian communities have clarified the differences between contending understandings in ways that manifestos and "conceptions of society" never could. In this practice of faithfulness may lie hope.

6

Church-Shaping Culture and Culture-Shaping Church

The Possibilities for a Christian Formative Project in America

While leaders and scholars in the church work at sorting out the nature of Christian involvement in public life and attempt to articulate coherent public theologies, "life goes on," and American public culture continues in its charted patterns. Public theologians offer the results of their analyses and their proposals to a pluralistic and contradictory culture. They speak within a culture that may lack the capacity to absorb and implement the full range of their foundational programs. It is a culture that needs demonstrations of faithfulness and consistency.

Contemporary public culture is the setting of the ongoing life and ministry of the church and inevitably contributes, however subtly, to the shaping of American churches, perhaps in ways contrary to the hopes of public theologians. Of course, it is possible that the church may be affecting public culture. Many analyses point to some of the ways in which the church has, and has not, shaped public culture and ways in which the church has been shaped by public culture. These measures may be anticipating some

133

profound challenges the church will face as it enters the next century, as they raise issues both for the central mission of the church and for the tensions the church will experience as it engages the culture. If these signs are true indicators, they also call for clear and careful thinking about any formative project the church may undertake. Can the church credibly hold forth a moral-cultural underpinning in this age? Is the culture able to absorb and adapt to such influence? Is the church able to offer a clear demonstration of consistency and faithfulness?

Among the most prominent characteristics of the American public, noted in previous chapters, are high levels of belief in God and reports of strong religious commitment and practice. The surveys cited in this book have discovered high levels of religious belief in the American public.[1] Yet a common observation is that these expressions of faith and commitment seem not to translate into equivalent commitments to public moral standards, or to affect political and social judgments at the levels we might expect. Shouldn't a highly religious people exhibit a more purposeful, moral, just, and peaceful public culture? Should not the church already have formed such a public culture?

Most observers agree that the church has not had this effect in contemporary America. Religion in general, while proliferating through the culture, seems to many to have little relevance to the dominant political, economic, and social forces shaping American culture at the end of the century. This general inference can also be drawn from analysis of survey data. For example, the levels of moral inconsistency and of moral-cultural diversity charted in chapter 4 exist in spite of the 90-percent-range agreement on the authority of the Bible and the general desire for moral cohesiveness within the public. Religious leaders must wonder what impact Christian truth is having on the ethics and lifestyles of those in their charge. Knowing, though, that these high levels of religiosity are general, not specific—in other words, that the American people are diverse in the content and organization of religious faith—it is worth exploring whether there are any sectors where religious commitment does make a difference. Because surveys sort Americans by religious category—evangelical, mainline Protestant, orthodox and progressive Catholic, secularist—we can look for patterns within these groups and compare them to the population as a whole. Further, we can ask whether any of these groups are particularly susceptible to the shaping influence of public culture.

One general observation from this pursuit is that, on the whole, the patterns of culture within religious groupings are much the same as those found in the overall public. But in some categories, religious conviction does make a difference. The most distinct differences are found among evangelicals and orthodox Catholics, who are more likely to oppose abortion, medical termination of life, adultery, sex education in schools, and the like; whereas secularists and mainline Christians are more likely to be tolerant of these. Americans also exhibit differences on specifically religious questions, such as on the authority of the Bible, personal relationship with God, prayer, and church attendance, with more conservative groups holding stronger views.

Table 6.1

Which of these statements comes closest to describing your feelings about the Bible:
(1) The Bible is the actual word of God, not mistaken in its statements and teaching, and is to be taken literally, word for word;
(2) The Bible is the inspired word of God, not mistaken in its teachings, but is not always to be taken literally, word for word;
(3) The Bible becomes the word of God for a person who reads it in faith;
(4) The Bible is an ancient book of legends, history, and moral precepts recorded by men.

		(1)	(2)	(3)	(4)
	Total population distribution	34%	32%	20%	13%
By ethnicity					
	African American	50	22	21	5
	Hispanic	37	30	22	10
	White	32	34	20	14
By gender					
	Female	37	30	20	12
	Male	32	34	20	14
By marital status					
	Single	30	34	19	16
	Married/1 marriage	34	34	20	12
	Married/2+ marriages	38	26	24	18
	Divorced/separated	31	26	24	18
By age					
	18–34	31	32	21	14
	35–49	31	34	21	13
	50–64	36	33	18	11
	65 or older	43	27	19	11

continued

		(1)	(2)	(3)	(4)
By region					
	East	20	43	20	15
	Midwest	27	37	24	12
	South	55	23	16	4
	West	28	27	21	24
By religion					
	Evangelical Protestant	66	21	13	1
	Mainline Protestant	25	37	25	13
	Orthodox Catholic	45	33	17	4
	Progressive Catholic	9	50	27	13
	Secularist	9	14	11	59
By education					
	Less than high school	53	18	19	9
	High school graduate	37	30	22	9
	Some college	32	35	20	12
	College graduate	17	39	21	22
	Post-graduate study	18	44	14	23
By social class					
	Poor laborer	45	18	21	13
	Low-mid income laborer	32	35	19	13
	Managers and entrepreneurs	30	34	25	10
	Professional	26	40	16	18
	Social elite	9	43	10	35
By political party					
	Democrat	39	29	18	13
	Republican	35	36	22	7
	Independent	26	32	22	18
By political interest level					
	High	28	35	20	17
	Moderate	34	34	20	12
	Low	42	27	21	8

This chapter goes beyond these specific questions to inquire whether particular religious commitment makes any difference in the development of a coherent public philosophy or in the more fundamental matters of underlying moral frameworks. Here we look again at the issues and trends established in part 1 of this book, sorting out the responses according to the religious categories reported in the demographic profile. The goal is to learn what part religious commitment has played in the formation of public culture, and whether particular religious beliefs make any difference in public attitudes and beliefs. Ultimately, we want to consider what type of formative project the church—or any sector of it—is capable of.

The entire American population is distributed generally in the following categories, according to survey response:

Evangelical Protestant	30%
Mainline Protestant	30
Orthodox Catholic	12
Progressive Catholic	20
Secularist	7
Other religions	1

These categories result primarily from self-reporting rather than examination of official membership figures. The definitions of these categories, however, correspond to common-sense perceptions. They of course will differ regionally and locally: for example, South Dakota will look very different from New York, or Florida from Idaho, in their distributions of religious affiliations as well as in ideological and partisan identifications.

The Impact of Postmodern Public Culture on the Church

As Christian leaders entertain hopes of shaping and guiding public culture, survey analyses offer some insight into the current level of influence that the church has on the culture and that culture has on the church. While it shows that formation is flowing in both directions, survey analyses make clear the powerful effect of contemporary culture on the life of the church. These data point to areas within the church that need attention if it is to lead and form public culture in the directions sketched out by public theologians. But the analyses do indicate some public concerns that may open up opportunities for Christian leadership even as the church struggles with the forces set against it.

The General Perception and Impact of the Gospel

The first observation builds on the already noted high level of belief in God and in the authority of the Bible to be found in public culture. Affirmations of these beliefs are reported in record numbers in recent surveys. Eighty-six percent of Americans say they believe the Bible is in some form the "Word of God." Further, most Americans hold their religious beliefs to be important, and most report attending religious services at least two to three times a month. Americans are personally religious people, and there is no doubt that the church and its teachings have had some degree of impact on the personal lives and habits of most Americans. Religion must be counted as one of the factors contributing to the shape of public culture.

Perhaps that influence has been one more of restraint than of positive culture building; in other words, since Americans can point to very few circumstances in which belief in God or the Bible directs their public decision making, religious belief may function more as a background or indirect influence that throws up barriers to excesses. Few Americans are conscious of God's authority or purpose in *public* life, and calls for public accountability to religious-based norms have few supporters in an atmosphere of demand for personal judgment and moral freedom. Religion is confined in great part to private belief and experience.

On the other hand, the high level of the public acceptance of religious belief calls into question the portents of strong antireligious moves or public persecution of Christians put forth by some Christian leaders. Religion is an acceptable factor in any contemporary "construction of identity" as long as it remains a personal matter and does not make public demands.

But the high degree of religious association among Americans and the high level of trust in religion may indicate that opportunities for leadership and influence are not completely absent. Americans at this moment still have confidence in their religious associations far beyond the levels given to other institutions, and they generally report satisfaction with the state of religion in the United States, again more than with other aspects of life. As other institutions falter, religious leadership still may retain a relatively strong opportunity to provide formative direction. That hope is of course weakened by the fact that the realm of religion is very diverse; a coordinated approach will be difficult to achieve. Further, influence and leadership must have a receptive audience, which may be the key missing element.

Prosperity and Satisfaction: Opportunity or Obstacle?

While the church has successfully contributed to the spread of belief throughout the culture, it has not injected any widespread motivations for cultural change or spiritual revival. Nor, in spite of high levels of public dissatisfaction, do survey analyses point to an impending spiritual crisis. One measure of the lack of interest for challenges by religious leadership may be found in the high levels among all Americans of personal satisfaction and personal prosperity and in the disconnection of these perceptions from public life, as explored earlier. These findings do not indicate a restless population seeking either spiritual revival or public reform. About 85 percent of Americans are either pleased or enthusiastic about their personal spiritual condition. Neither the essential message of the gospel, the call to repentance, nor a demand for public accountability to higher norms will resonate broadly throughout the public. Under these conditions, any support for political or social change will have to come from commitment to principles rather than from responses to personal threats or fears of direct impact from public challenges.

The happy and satisfied public mood not only makes the soil less receptive to the seeds of the gospel; it also subtly shapes the life of the church itself. This may help explain why the prevailing mode of the church in the 1990s was to be seeker-friendly, nonthreatening, and nondoctrinaire. Church becomes another piece in the overall happiness puzzle, perhaps even contributing to the general level of contentment through a message adapted to that mood rather than making hard moral-cultural demands.

These changes are well-documented and encouraged by many leaders and missiologists. Others are less enthusiastic, lamenting the corrosive effects on the church in this environment. Writing in the May 11, 1997, *Washington Post,* Presbyterian pastor Henry Brinton tells about his congregation:

> Calvary Presbyterian Church is not a user-friendly name for a congregation, and this puts my church at a distinct disadvantage in today's Christian marketplace. Many people, especially adults born after 1945, shop for the church that is most convenient, comfortable and satisfying for them. These shoppers have little denominational loyalty or sense of obligation to any particular community of faith. Instead, they are drawn to churches that have plenty of parking, attractive facilities and programs that promise to meet their spiritual needs. Researchers such as Dean Hoge of Catholic University have found that many baby boomers are looking for "high-quality Sunday school

and youth programs, uplifting worship experiences and meaningful, authentic small-group experiences." . . .

Into this economy have stepped such full-service churches as the Christian Center [nearby]. This nondenominational congregation offers contemporary praise and worship, drama, and special ministries for singles, children and youths. As a seven-day-a-week church, its activities go far beyond Sunday worship: There are Saturday prayer groups and Wednesday evening classes, as well as weekday Christian school and opportunities for mission trips. The church even offers country and western dance lessons![2]

In spite of the public mood of satisfaction, however, an opportunity for Christian leadership may come from the contradiction between public and private levels of satisfaction. Having achieved the goals of personal happiness in this time of prosperity and having made other institutions—including religious ones—part of that pursuit, Americans may turn their attention to conforming government and public life, with which they are not satisfied, to their happiness. This may force a moment of crisis into which effective leadership can step, although a dangerous moment, since the mood will not necessarily be receptive to philosophy or right public order but will be aimed toward seeking satisfaction. Anticipating this moment and preparing for it could be the primary task for Christian leadership committed to the formative project. Such a time of crisis could provide opportunity to articulate and demonstrate the true purposes and goals of citizenship rather than pander to selfish pursuits.

Another possibility: if the gulf widens between this settled sense of personal and family life on the one hand and perceptions of alien and hostile values among cultural elites on the other, perhaps Americans will increase the pressure on those elites and on public culture. The demand for "family values" in this sense may intensify the climate of cultural crisis and provide the opportunity for effective leadership. Religious leaders, as those who ought to be most familiar with the priority of family and community well-being, could provide this leadership. Thus while the climate may not suggest impending demands for spiritual revival, given the high level of personal spiritual satisfaction, an effort to bring public culture closer to the central values and concerns of Americans may have some possibility of success in the prevailing public mood.

The Effects of Dualism on the Life of the Church

Previous chapters explored the extent to which Americans hold contradictory moral concepts simultaneously and examined how conflicts among these concepts can cause public confusion. Americans feel tension between commitments to community and public associations and to their individual interests and pursuits. They are unclear about the public application of absolute values versus tolerating a high level of personal freedom. Just as this has an effect on public life, as explored, the question has to arise: In what ways will these public tendencies affect the teachings and practices of the church?

Will church identity and participation drop in the new century, as it already has among other associations? Will Americans, in their general retreat into private life, finally also withdraw from this last arena where membership is still very high? It could be that religious associations will eventually go the way of other community connections. This may turn in great part on the leadership question. If Americans continue to have little confidence in political leaders and other elites, they may stick with religious leaders as their last hope for trust and guidance. The spiritual dimension of religious association may give extra reinforcement to these connections in ways not available to other leaders. On the other hand, if religious leaders also lose the confidence of the American people—through scandal, irrelevancy, folly, and the like—Americans may complete the trend to privatization by giving up on religious connections also.

The prevailing public moral uncertainty may shape the internal life of the church as well, as it subtly adapts. In the search for ways to serve and lead, religious leaders may tend to avoid demands that could drive members away and to accommodate to the fuzzy public mood. Definitive declarations will be avoided, since they cannot be understood or adopted by hearers. The New Testament call to authoritative, sacramental community is a difficult one for this ambivalent culture. There are few with ears to hear such messages, even though most Americans are involved in churches to some degree. Henry Brinton's appeal may make sense to fewer Americans as time passes:

If preachers lose their prophetic edge, and focus on comfort to the exclusion of challenge, then the church has become nothing more than another self-help group. People should have their legitimate needs met, but they should also be challenged to confess their sins, be reconciled to one another, listen for God's Word, and then do good work in the world. Jesus did not ask people to choose him and use him; instead he called men and women to follow him in a ministry of service to a troubled world. . . . Maybe such a mission is the commodity that young adults are really looking for as they shop and hop from church to church.[3]

The Effects of Dualism on Coherent Public Philosophy

American public ambivalence joins experiential pluralism to form the primary cultural obstacles to the cultivation of coherent public philosophy in the United States. This will be no less true for a formative Christian project. As with the effects on the internal life of churches, Christian demands for coherence in public life will also meet this contemporary American mood of "having it all" and "keeping options open." The soil appears to be hard and unyielding for the planting of the public life implications of the gospel.

On the other hand, it can be said that these expressions of ambivalence may contain a cry for clarity. In one survey, in the midst of the clear resistance to choosing the common good or moral absolutes for guidance, three-quarters of Americans agreed that "we would all be better off if we could live by the same basic moral guidelines." Perhaps the moral ambivalence comes from the absence of a convincing common morality. A persuasive authority may be able to capture this public desire and win the hearts of Americans. Christian leaders will want to hope that it is their truth-based formation that is persuasive, rather than the messages of demagogues or tyrants. They will also want to plow ahead in their calling to lead, even if success is uncertain.

Shaping of Values: Does Religion Make a Difference?

In pursuing the questions of what forms the moral framework in America and to what degree the moral and public culture in the United States has impact on the church, it is noteworthy that Americans with religious commitments generally follow the same patterns as Americans as a whole. The differences on most public questions—and in the expression of a common political philosophy or rudimentary moral framework—between the various religious categories are insignificant. On some essential matters, however, there are significant differences between the perceptions of those with specific religious commitments and the general public.

The strongest differences were between evangelicals and secularists, and between each of these and the general public. The differences are not found in the areas of political beliefs, trust in leaders, or general commitments to rights and American ideals. All categories of Americans showed similar views on these matters. Rather, the most pronounced differences are in the degree of intensity with which perceptions are held by these groups and in their disagreements on certain social trends and moral questions. In these areas, evangelicals alone have largely, though not completely, gone different routes than the public culture.

For example, evangelicals agreed with other Americans that the nation is in decline, but they held those views to a greater extent than the aggregate (64 percent of evangelicals versus 52 percent of all Americans). They were more dissatisfied with public life and more likely to perceive strong decline in various institutions and aspects of American life. They were especially strong on perceiving decline in family life, in moral and ethical standards, and in national spiritual life. On questions of approval of recent social changes, evangelicals were stronger in disapproval, while secularists were stronger in approval, of such controversial matters as acceptance of homosexuality. Evangelicals were more intensely worried about the future of the nation and about the future of family life and morality than their fellow citizens. Evangelicals far outdistanced other groups, however, in agreeing that "America is the greatest country in the world," indicating that as a group their expectations run very high.

Table 6.2

Patriotism versus Satisfaction
Is the U.S. the greatest country in the world?

	General	Evangelicals	Secularists
(% saying yes)	55%	68%	46%
Are you satisfied or dissatisfied with how things are going in the U.S.?			
(% somewhat or very dissatisfied)	58	71	50

Table 6.3

Perceptions of Decline
Percentage in each category indicating strong or moderate decline
(**bold** indicates strong category difference)

	General	Evangelicals	Secularists
U.S. as a nation	53%	**64%**	50%
Standard of living	54	56	54
Education and schools	61	63	60

continued

	General	Evangelicals	Secularists
Family life	64	**72**	63
Work ethic	56	**64**	48
Moral and ethical standards	70	**78**	62
Quality of TV/entertainment	71	**82**	56
Crime/public safety	73	**83**	73
Religious/spiritual life	43	**52**	40
Business and economy	48	53	45
Racial/ethnic relations	45	43	**51**
Criminal justice system	67	71	66
Health care system	56	55	**70**
Quality of national leaders	57	64	66
Military power	27	31	27
Churches/religious institutions	29	36	27
Honesty/integrity of Americans	50	56	50

Other differences appeared when Americans were asked what steps should be taken to improve life in the United States. Again, evangelicals and secularists differed drastically on certain approaches, while they were similar to each other and to the rest of the population on other means. Evangelicals to a much greater degree than others believed improvements would occur if more parents spanked their children for discipline, if traditional values were taught in schools, if religion were allowed in public schools, if mothers did not work and stayed home with their children, if society were less materialistic, if more people focused on their families, and especially, if more people went to church. Secularists were much closer to the views of the general population, except on going to church, where only 18 percent thought it would help the country, whereas 40 percent of all Americans surveyed (and 63 percent of evangelicals) thought it would help.

Surprisingly, in light of the findings that distinguish evangelicals (and, on a few issues, orthodox Catholics) in moral and social patterns from the rest of the population, they are very similar to all Americans in their contradictory decision-making tendencies. *Evangelicals agreed in the same high levels as the general population that "values are something that each of us must decide without being influenced by others," and that "what is true for me is not necessarily true for others."* They do stand out for agreeing far more than the general population that "those who violate God's rules will be punished." Secularists of course showed little agreement with this last statement. Further, secularists also showed lower levels of agreement than the whole survey that "we would all be better off if we lived by the same basic moral guidelines," whereas evangelicals were slightly more in agreement with this than the general population. More clearly, on the question, "If you were unsure of what was right or wrong, which would be the most important in deciding what you would do?" 57 percent of evangelicals chose following what "God or Scripture" directed, as opposed to 26 percent of the general population. Evangelicals alone, then, are *relatively* more firm in moral notions than the wider public culture, though they also show signs of the cultural ambiguity found at large.

Evangelicals stand out even more clearly in questions related to specific issues. They alone answered in large percentages that the following were "wrong for all": premarital sex, homosexual sex, homosexual marriage, taking drugs, consuming pornography, and the medical termination of life. Evangelicals were the only group that both condemned abortion and wanted it illegal; even Catholics, while condemning the practice, were less willing to make it subject to legal penalty.

Abortion is the clearest case to be drawn from survey data in which religion makes a difference in dealing with public questions. The following table details the responses by religious category to the question of the moral evaluation of abortion.

Table 6.4

Which of these statements comes closest to describing your feelings about abortion:
(1) Abortion is just as bad as killing a person who has already been born—it is murder;
(2) Abortion is murder, but it is not as bad as killing someone who has already been born;
(3) Abortion is not murder, but it does involve the taking of human life;
(4) Abortion is not murder—it is a surgical procedure for removing human tissue.

	(1)	(2)	(3)	(4)
Total population distribution	38%	10%	26%	16%
By ethnicity				
African American	40	9	15	17
Hispanic	49	13	22	9
White	36	9	28	17
By gender				
Female	39	8	27	16
Male	37	12	24	15
By marital status				
Single	33	10	25	18
Married/1 marriage	42	10	25	13

continued

	(1)	(2)	(3)	(4)
Married/2+ marriages	35	9	33	18
Divorced/separated	28	9	30	19
By age				
18–34	34	10	31	14
35–49	36	10	28	16
50–64	46	10	16	16
65 or older	41	10	21	16
By region				
East	37	13	25	16
Midwest	39	7	30	14
South	43	12	22	11
West	30	7	28	24
By religion				
Evangelical Protestant	58	10	16	7
Mainline Protestant	28	8	31	19
Orthodox Catholic	54	9	23	6
Progressive Catholic	33	15	31	11
Secularist	6	5	28	45
By education				
Less than high school	49	10	18	11
High school graduate	40	12	24	13
Some college	36	8	28	27
College graduate	30	9	28	27
Post-graduate study	26	10	35	19
By social class				
Poor laborer	47	8	18	12
Low-mid income laborer	34	11	30	15
Managers and entrepreneurs	43	9	28	13
Professional	36	12	26	18
Social elite	26	4	27	35
By political party				
Democrat	36	9	25	19
Republican	46	10	27	11
Independent	33	11	27	17
By political interest level				
High	34	10	29	19
Moderate	37	10	25	17
Low	44	10	21	10

From *The Public Perspective*, February/March 1997

Evangelicals thus seem to have the strongest claim to being distinct from the general relativism and ambiguity of the wider American public culture. Even they, however, are not wholly distinct; they show many of the same tendencies towards uncertainty. Religion does make some difference in shaping public philosophy, but only for some Americans. That American evangelicals are distinct of course points both to their greater level of resistance to the trends in public culture, but it also points to the fact that they have not influenced public culture with their perspectives to any great degree. Yet the differences between evangelicals and secularists still point to the strongest rival visions posed for the direction of American culture in the new century.

Differentiated Responsibility

In searching for some operating political philosophy at work in guiding American political culture, surveys reveal that most Americans do not hold a differentiated concept of public responsibility. When asked who was responsible for a range of public problems from among federal, state, and local governments, private organizations, and individuals, most Americans chose some level of government as the primary entity. This was true even on the questions of financing a college education, providing health care, and "deciding when prayer is permissible in public schools." The striking finding in this inquiry is how little support Americans had for private organizations as the responsible actors on public problems. In this land of voluntary organizations, the expectations for associations are very low.

Table 6.5

Evangelical "Statism"

Should the following public concerns be mainly the responsibility of the federal government, state government, local government, private organizations, or individuals? (Percentages of all evangelical Americans)

Issue	Federal Govt.	State Govt.	Local Govt.	Private Orgs.	Individuals
Protect environment	55%	24%	10%	6%	6%
Fair treatment of women/minorities	67	13	12	3	6
Health standards for meat and dairy	71	18	6	4	1
National security	92	5	2	0	0
Help poor and unemployed	38	36	13	7	6

continued

Issue	Federal Govt.	State Govt.	Local Govt.	Private Orgs.	Individuals
Finance college education	28	23	4	10	35
Guard against hiring discrimination	52	26	12	6	4
Setting workplace safety standards	50	27	14	8	2
Decide when school prayer is permissible	25	25	20	2	28
Setting educational standards	27	44	20	2	18
Permitting smoking in public places	26	24	26	7	18
Feeding poorest Americans	56	18	13	8	6
Financing health care	59	18	5	5	13
Mean	49.7	23.1	12.1	5.2	10.2

Table 6.6

Secularist "Statism"

Should the following public concerns be mainly the responsibility of the federal government, state government, local government, private organizations, or individuals? (Percentages of all secularist Americans)

Issue	Federal Govt.	State Govt.	Local Govt.	Private Orgs.	Individuals
Protect environment	81%	13%	2%	4%	1%
Fair treatment of women/minorities	64	19	5	3	10
Health standards for meat and dairy	76	17	6	1	1
National security	89	6	4	1	0
Help poor and unemployed	42	34	18	2	4
Finance college education	32	21	8	9	29
Guard against hiring discrimination	52	30	8	5	4
Setting workplace safety standards	54	22	15	7	4
Decide when school prayer is permissible	31	13	22	5	29
Setting educational standards	30	49	15	1	6
Permitting smoking in public places	17	27	25	10	21
Feeding poorest Americans	57	20	18	3	3
Financing health care	62	20	6	5	7
Mean	49.7	23.1	12.1	5.2	10.2

Religious affiliation made no perceptible difference in these expectations. Even evangelicals, who stand out for a few stronger moral convictions and policy prescriptions, as noted, are only marginally different on these matters. Even on the matter of who is to decide when prayer is "permissible" in public schools—that is, when and if someone should pray—most evangelicals saw this as a legal or policy question rather than a matter for personal choice: 25 percent of evangelicals indicated the federal government,

25 percent state governments, 20 percent local governments, 2 percent private organizations, and 28 percent indicated it should be left to individuals. Evangelicals gave responses similar to those of the rest of the population on the other public concerns tested as well: namely, that government has primary responsibility.

While evangelicals exhibit strong positions on some moral and public issues, they do not then go to the next step of holding a Christian-based, pluralistic concept of public responsibility. Generalized, practical statism is evident in their public expectations to the same degree that it is in the general population—though it is even higher for secularists. The agendas of active evangelical political groups reflect this, with their strong emphasis on national and state legislative policy and on court decisions. Evangelicals do show a slightly higher desire to "reduce the size of the federal government" than the general population, but they do not then demonstrate a clear idea of the shift of responsibilities to other sectors. Their higher disaffection and even delegitimization of the national government has not yet been translated into a consensus on a different way of public life, certainly not into a concept that is based on pluralistic, associational responsibility.

Robert Putnam comments on this characteristic of evangelicals, based on his extensive survey data:

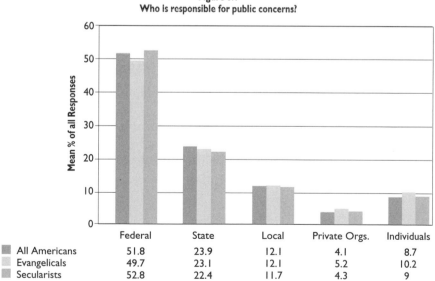

Figure 6.1
Who is responsible for public concerns?

	Federal	State	Local	Private Orgs.	Individuals
All Americans	51.8	23.9	12.1	4.1	8.7
Evangelicals	49.7	23.1	12.1	5.2	10.2
Secularists	52.8	22.4	11.7	4.3	9

Both individually and congregationally, evangelicals are more likely to be involved in activities within their own religious community but are less likely to be involved in the broader community. Evangelicals attend church more regularly . . . , are far more generous philanthropically . . . , and have more close friends in the same congregation. . . . The social capital of evangelicals, however, is invested at home more than in the wider community. Among evangelicals, church attendance is *not* correlated with membership in community organizations. . . . Most evangelical volunteering . . . supports the religious life of the congregation itself . . . but does not extend to the broader community as much as volunteering by members of other faiths.[4]

Therefore, if a differentiated public philosophy is to be the effect of a Christian formative project, it may need to begin within the church before it seeks to have influence on the wider culture.

Compartmentalized Religion

It is the case at the beginning of the twenty-first century that while religion is still an important feature of American life and has some influence on public culture, that influence is limited to certain issues and to specific groups of Americans. Even after some decades of intense and well-organized Christian public activism, the majority of Americans still does not receive its political guidance from religious leadership or even from a general sense of religious moral guidance. Americans retain the right of personal judgment in moral and public questions. While over 90 percent of Americans believe in God, according to survey data, only 26 percent say they would do "what God or Scripture tells you is right" when "unsure of what is right or wrong."

Religion makes a difference in expected categories, such as certain moral questions and personal philosophies, but not in general political and public life categories. Religious commitment, especially among evangelicals, is a factor in resistance to the effects of some cultural trends on the church. This study shows empirically that it is the case, as some evangelical Christians say they have experienced, that American culture is different from and at times antagonistic toward their values.

Religion does make a difference, according to some commentators, in general behavior that has public impact. For example, Robin Gill, in *Church-*

going and Christian Ethics, concludes that "churchgoers have, in addition to their distinctive theistic and christocentric beliefs, a strong sense of moral order and concern for other people,"[5] and participate more often in voluntary social activities than nonchurchgoers. In the oft-cited *Bowling Alone,* Robert Putnam cites numerous studies in drawing the conclusion that (nonevangelical) churchgoers in the United States are "substantially more likely to be involved in secular organizations, vote and participate politically in other ways, and have deeper social connections."[6] David Myers, in *The American Paradox,* also refers to studies showing that juveniles who attend church are "much less likely to become delinquent, to engage in promiscuous sex, and to abuse alcohol and drugs."[7] Yet these general and positive effects of religious affiliation on citizenship, not to be ignored or disregarded, have not translated into a thorough and comprehensive public philosophy.

It is clearly also the case that comprehensive Christian public philosophies advanced by their advocates have made little headway in forming a general cultural understanding. The limited distinctions associated with religious commitment are overshadowed by the moral pluralism of the United States. The various moral-cultural clusters found in the United States are more significant indicators of political orientation and moral framework than is religious belief. These cultural divisions exist in spite of the saturation of America by religious teaching and the pervasiveness of religious belief to be found in the United States. Religion is one factor in the formation of those orientations, but the scope of the clusters indicates that the major religious communities in the United States each contain at least some representation from the variety of moral orientations.

Even evangelicals, the most distinct group, do not widely show evidence of any of the criteria for a robust public philosophy that we have explored. If anything, evangelicals are even more alienated from leadership structures, more hostile to constitutive authority, and more withdrawn from public life into family life and church life, conceived of as private and "spiritual," than other Americans. Some have been motivated to pursue public leadership in this context, as the rise of the Christian Coalition, the success of evangelical and Catholic candidates, and the growth of evangelical political activism at all levels of government attest. But the limited impact of these efforts on public culture, as well as the interactive effects of public culture on the life and doctrine of the church, suggests that the opportunities for effective direct action are limited. As Americans "keep their options open," Christian leadership is not completely closed out; but any formative project will entail laborious and extended effort and will require long-term consistency in vision and in practical wisdom as the church faithfully lives out its calling. Perhaps leadership is most needed at the level of pre-formation—cultivating the life of the church as the ground in which an enriched public life can grow.

7

Obstacles and Opportunities for Christians in the Twenty-First Century

Son of man, say to Pharaoh king of Egypt and to his multitude: "Whom are you like in your greatness? Behold, I will liken you to a cedar in Lebanon, with fair branches and forest shade, and of great height, its top among the clouds. . . . So it towered high above all the trees of the forest; its boughs grew large and its branches long, from abundant water in its shoots. All the birds of the air made their nests in its boughs; under its branches all the beasts of the field brought forth their young; and under its shadow dwelt all great nations. . . . I made it beautiful in the mass of its branches, and all the trees of Eden envied it, that were in the garden of God.

Therefore thus says the Lord God: Because it towered high and set its top among the clouds, and its heart was proud of its height, I will give it into the hand of a mighty one of the nations; he shall surely deal with it as its wickedness deserves. I have cast it out. Foreigners, the most terrible of the nations, will cut it down and leave it. On the mountains and in all the valleys its branches will fall, and its boughs will lie broken in all the watercourses of the land; and all the peoples of the earth will go from its shadow and leave it. Upon its ruin will dwell all the birds of the air, and upon its branches will be all the beasts of the field. All this in order that no trees by the water may grow to lofty height or set their tops among the clouds, and that no trees that drink water may reach up to them in height; for they all are given over to death, to the nether world among mortal men, with those who go down to the Pit."

Ezekiel 31:2–14

Paradigm Shifts and New Realities

If the reflections of political theologians such as Oliver O'Donovan are right, that a society is judged by its faithfulness in rightly constituting authority and structuring its common life under the ultimate authority of God's law, then by virtue of their vocation, Christian leaders have a social and public role as well as an ecclesiastical role. As those with access to the content of divine standards and faith in their Author, Christians contribute to society with their faith and knowledge. Christian leaders understand that earthly authority is ultimately derived not from a social contract or human intention but from creation and common grace and that it is subject to heavenly order and law.

But Christian leaders also undertake their public responsibilities fully aware that American public culture is receptive to neither clear moral authority nor to the primacy of community commitments, nor even to credible public leadership. However, if American culture is not receptive to the formative effects of a comprehensive, articulated public philosophy, it may be receptive to a credible demonstration of committed public life. But even the work of providing such a demonstration may be beyond the current capacity of the American church, given its own incoherence and public uncertainties, as previous chapters have shown.

Obstacles, however, are no excuse not to be faithful to responsibility. The calling of Christian leadership is now to be carried out in the world in which we live; this is a given, even though we know full well that the cultural context itself is part of what has to be led and influenced. The disaffection of

Americans with their political system is a portent of demands for change, joining the effects of larger economic, technological, and international changes in suggesting that the next century will see significant redefinitions of the American experiment. The combined effect of these pressures means that a critical occasion for leadership is approaching, and the church must prepare for it.

As leaders engage in any project that hopes for public effects, they will have to account for the cultural divisions in American society. They must understand and speak to the diverse moral-cultural segments of the United States in comprehensible ways. Certain demands will be less tenable to some Americans than others. Those who are permissive in orientation, for example, are unlikely to accept any effort to define absolute rules for personal behavior; traditionalists will resist pressure to accept public toleration of certain behaviors. The currently visible contentious issues—such as abortion, assisted suicide, embryonic stem cell research, funding of faith-based organizations, school vouchers, school prayer, and the like—will not offer arenas for public consensus. Therefore a formative project would seek to lead Americans toward some common commitments in spite of their differences, and to a sense of public authority and responsibility that enables public faithfulness to divine norms.

Many questions remain, however. As new circumstances show, the formative project cannot be simply restorative in nature. It is not a matter of restoring certain values to public life or of recovering a lost sense of common purpose. The American dreams of exceptional prosperity, global leadership, and resisting tyranny were formative myths of other ages. A cohesive public culture and philosophy for the new century will not be nostalgic. It will not merely evoke times when cultural consensus was greater, when Christianity was dominant, when communities were more tightly knit—though these may provide reference points for Christian leadership. As the examination of contemporary Christian attempts to address public life has shown, pluralism—ethnic, moral, and political—requires us to account for many new factors and circumstances. These circumstances bring challenges to the traditional concepts of public life advanced by the church in the past and to those now being put forth. Yet they offer opportunities for Christian influence, in word and deed, that could bring hope and some order to public life.

*The Changing Organization of Power: The End
of Modernity and Structural Pluralism*

One major challenge the church must face as it engages public life is to discern exactly what is the *object* of a formative project. What is the entity that constitutes "the public"? A public philosophy of responsibility, authority, and community must have some sense of the location of those qualities. For 350 years, the global pattern of the modern age has been the formation and maintenance of sovereign states or nation-states. The concept of the state is clearly a construct of the modern era, a self-contained, rational, structured, clearly defined entity with a common language, culture, and territory. We generally have known what we mean by the "United States of America" or any other national identification. Many indicators suggest, however, that the state as we have known it is changing drastically and that public identity and authority are developing new forms and new locations. Will it be sufficient to focus public influence on "America," as we have defined the union since the Civil War?

"I would guess that the interest of political theorists over the next decades will lie, as it were, above and below the level of the nation (and the nation-state). It will lie in transnational formations of different sorts and in civil society."[1] Political philosopher Michael Walzer's remarks point to two trends that are disrupting the established concept that identifies community with nation-state: rising levels of international cooperation and integration, on the one hand, and the increasing power of subnational governments and nongovernmental institutions on the other, challenge the comfortable statism of much political thinking. In a sense, the differentiation promoted by many Christian thinkers is being accomplished through technological and economic change as trade, security, and even social regulations are internationalized. At the same time, in the United States and elsewhere, budget pressures and difficulties associated with sustaining nationwide services are resulting in the devolution of responsibility to state and local governments and other institutions.

The formation of a moral and responsible citizenry, then, must consider all these levels of power. The effort must first of all either validate or invalidate these trends: Do we really approve of and support the increasing economic regulatory power of the World Trade Organization? Or the requirements of international consultation and legitimization before we employ military force? Do we want states and localities determining welfare, education, and environmental standards? Surveys of American political culture show that Americans still have high levels of expectation for the national government in public matters—as opposed to other governments and private organizations—contrary to these trends. Do Americans need to be led to a more robust and pluralistic concept of public authority? How will we account for these realities in the new century if we remain state-centric?

Further, how can we determine the legitimacy of authority and hold it accountable if it is so diffuse? It is clear that a singular focus on national community and government must be given up. Formation efforts cannot simply seek to cultivate good citizenship for the state. The current disaffection with the national government may be explained in part by the high expectations for it that cannot be achieved in this changing environment. National government alone cannot change economic circumstances, ensure quality of life and health, and provide excellent education, let alone improve the moral and spiritual life of Americans.

Understanding these multiple centers of power and authority will not only require clear justification but will also elaborate complex means of participation and accountability. For example, it is possible to see the hand of Providence in diffusing earthly authority into multiple forms as a check on tyranny and other forms of human sin. Further, it should be possible to clarify the expectations for different levels of power in ways appropriate to their nature—as in the claim that limited international authority may be necessary to uphold universal standards of human rights and dignity in this age of globalization. And cooperative international economic arrangements could foster greater levels of provision for the poor if they are not overtaken by selfish interests. At the same time, participatory and immediate avenues for dealing with local needs, as mundane as they are, can offer direct means for citizens to serve each other publicly and should not be surrendered to impersonal international power structures.

Michael Sandel advocates such an understanding in his call for the revitalization of public philosophy in the global age:

> The cosmopolitan vision is wrong to suggest that we can restore self-government simply by pushing sovereignty and citizenship upward. The hope for self-government lies not in relocating sovereignty but in dispersing it. The most promising alternative to the sovereign state is not a one-world community based on the solidarity of humankind, but a multiplicity of communities and political bodies—some more, some less extensive than

nations—among which sovereignty is diffused. The nation-state need not fade away, only cede its claim as the sole repository of sovereign power and primary object of political allegiance. Different forms of political association would govern different spheres of life and engage different aspects of our identities. Only a regime that disperses sovereignty both upward and downward can combine the power required to rival global market forces with the differentiation required of a public life that hopes to inspire the reflective allegiance of its citizens.[2]

A Christian perspective will also place checks on expectations for global society. The global level of organization can never displace national and local authorities or unify them into one grand authority. Such would be Babel-like idolatry and come under judgment. The state is not disappearing but changing, weakening only relatively while retaining substantial power. Further, global governance is also subject to something higher. Oliver O'Donovan notes in his careful study of the nature of the earthly implications of the Kingdom of God that

> the rule of Yhwh was conceived internationally: it secured the relations of the nations and directed them towards peace. But at the international level there was to be no unitary mediator. . . . Yhwh's world order was plurally constituted. World-empire was a bestial deformation. . . . To propose a generalised statement: *the appropriate unifying element in international order is law rather than government.*[3]

As written law is the appropriate, Biblical form for articulating the means of obedience to true authority (rather than direct mediation through human leaders), this must also be true internationally if there is to be legitimate international authority. International authority must be limited and directed toward specific ends.

A credible formative public philosophy will develop a clear understanding of these realities, indicate how people connect to them, and grasp the nature of law and authority at all levels in this diverse context. The church, as a transnational, catholic reality that nevertheless takes shape in local and diverse forms, understands and experiences such plurality. It also understands the supreme providential source of law and the universal obligation to it. The church has experienced divisions and contentions over many issues, yet it maintains a common identity to a common Lord and a common commitment to his will being done on earth as it is in heaven. The reflections of the church may be even more pertinent to the emerging political situation in the twenty-first century than they have been since the Middle Ages, when the idea of universal spiritual authority sustained the concept of human unity in a situation of cultural and political fluidity. Perhaps the church can restore a common human understanding of essential standards if it can renew that understanding within itself as it seeks good order and righteous living for human beings.

Adjustments in Secular Structure:
The End of Modernity and Cultural Pluralism

Along with facing the changing nature of the state and the redistribution of political power, a Christian contribution to public formation must also address other adjustments occurring in the post–Cold War, postmodern period in public life. The ideological battles of the twentieth century have given way to other challenges to order. Conflicts between fascism, communism, capitalism, and liberalism are being replaced by different forms of conflict, given the major geopolitical changes of the 1990s. Many have written about these changes, and public discourse is inundated with this discussion.[4]

These changes are also connected with intellectual challenges to the legitimacy of the prevailing ideas of modernity—the beliefs in technological and social progress, scientific reasoning, and rational structuring of human community in the form of the state. The modern materialistic ideologies that guided the primary political questions of the twentieth century are declining in power, not only through their own failures but also because scholars, as well as the public, have come to find their premises unconvincing. These premises have been in large degree undermined by human experience in the twentieth century—as all the scientific "progress" in the world has also brought mass destruction and invasive technology—and by the sweeping results of developments among intellectuals. Philosopher Richard Rorty, who is most often cited on these matters, welcomes the passing of foundationalism—the concept that certain fundamental ideas are both verifiable and necessary to human life. He calls for the abandonment of this impulse and the embrace of relativism:

> As I see it, one important intellectual advance which has been made in our
> century is . . . a growing willingness to neglect the question "What is our
> nature?" and to substitute the question "What can we make of ourselves?"
> We are much less inclined than our ancestors were to take "theories of human
> nature" seriously, much less inclined to take ontology or history [or ideol-
> ogy] as a guide to life. We have come to see that the only lesson of either his-
> tory or anthropology is our extraordinary malleability. We are coming to
> think of ourselves as the flexible, protean, self-shaping animal rather than as
> the rational animal or the cruel animal.[5]

This move to fluidity of course applies to the abandonment of religious
foundations as well as rationalistic and scientific foundations for conduct-
ing our lives.

Whether or not Americans have fully abandoned foundationalism, as
Rorty hopes, it is the case that the rationalistic formulations of the twentieth century no longer have the same power they once may have held. A
Christian formative project will not, then, set about a defensive or reactive
course. It will not be satisfied with putting forth an "alternative theistic ideology" or attempting to provide a point-for-point response to secularism,
as if good ideas will be sufficient. American public culture is not capable of
absorbing and accepting such a set of propositions.

The sense of openness (that Rorty depicts as "malleability") brought by
the loss of faith in progress and ideology need not point, however, to an era
of despair, vulnerability, or fear. It could anticipate a more robust and adven-
turous time of cultural development and even of religious power. The new
era could be a time to go beyond making a Christian "case" for or against
capitalism, socialism, or democracy. It is indeed a time for fresh thinking
and fresh modes of action. Of course, this hope of opportunity does not
necessarily guarantee a time of stability or success for formative projects, as
other competitors in the formation contest will also emerge.

One scenario presented by Harvard political scientist Samuel Huntington
for the emerging postmodern global public order is that new forms of political and cultural organization are emerging from the demise of ideological
modernity, taking shape in the more traditional category of "civilizations."

> In the late 1980s the communist world collapsed, and the Cold War inter-
> national system became history. In the post-Cold War world, the most impor-
> tant distinctions among peoples are not ideological, political, or economic.

They are cultural. Peoples and nations are attempting to answer the most basic question humans face: Who are we? And they are answering that question in the traditional way human beings have answered it, by reference to the things that mean the most to them. People define themselves in terms of ancestry, religion, language, history, values, customs, and institutions. They identify with cultural groups: tribes, ethnic groups, religious communities, nations, and at the broadest level, civilizations. People use politics not just to advance their interests but also to define their identity. We know who we are only when we know who we are not and often only when we know whom we are against.[6]

Huntington's thesis points us again to the significance of culture in the consciousness of people and to its operation as a primary factor in political life. While thicker, cultural connections may have been hidden in the recent past by ideological conflict, they will now emerge more prominently. Public formation, in this age when modern paradigms and ideologies have declined in influence, is more open to understanding the complexities of culture. Further, cultures themselves can become the focus of public formation, since they change over time and may be subject to influence and direction.

A related issue in contemporary public formation, then, is the need to deal with the matter of rising nationalism, which at first glance may appear to contradict the trend toward broader civilizational identity. Yet according to Huntington, nationalistic conflicts are local expressions of the broader civilizational forces and are enabled by the decline of modern systems. These loyalties will be strong challengers to any Christian formative vision. Nationalism arises when a group rubs against another very different group. "Civilization and culture both refer to the overall way of life of a people, and a civilization is a culture writ large. They both involve the 'values, norms, institutions, and modes of thinking to which successive generations in a given society have attached primary importance.'"[7] Huntington expects the emerging primacy of civilizations to result in widespread conflict, perhaps even within the United States, as we become more diverse. "In this new world the most pervasive, important, and dangerous conflicts will not be between social classes, rich and poor, or other economically defined groups, but between peoples belonging to different cultural entities."[8] Can a Christian formative project accommodate these differences while also structuring means of peaceful interaction and resolution of conflicts? Should these differences be affirmed or must they be overcome through adoption of a new universal foundation?

Whether or not the civilization paradigm becomes the overall guiding mode for political organization and conflict, a number of effects may result from these new trends. One is the degree to which community and culture are figuring in the development of personal identity for many people, suggesting that many Americans have found limits to extreme individualism. To the degree that American democracy is built on individualistic notions of rights and participation, it may experience significant challenge. The ambivalence over whether the community or the individual has priority, fully expressed in surveys of American political culture, may indicate a trend in the United States similar to what has been seen elsewhere: a move toward more particular forms of community identity. Accounting for these identities politically will require mechanisms of participation different from those based on individual choice. The growing demand in the United States for proportional representation and multiple parties is one way some analysts and activists have begun to respond to these trends.[9]

With the decline of ideological modernism, the reemergence of culture forces a new look at the entire idea of "America" and "American culture." Among those who consider themselves advocates of community (or "communitarians"), there is disagreement between those who believe that a large political entity, such as the United States, can sustain the moral and other connections to be a cohesive nation (for example, Amitai Etzioni, Jean Bethke Elshtain, Michael Sandel) and others who believe that culture is more cohesive in smaller units reinforced by language, history, connections to land, and common experiences (Wendell Berry, Richard Weaver, and various "agrarians"). According to Wendell Berry, "Culture preserves the map and the records of past journeys so that no generation will permanently destroy the route. The more local and settled the culture, the better it stays put, the less the damage."[10] Such debates are at the root of tensions in many nation-states currently experiencing internal separatist movements, such as Canada, the United Kingdom, Spain, and Russia; these debates could foreshadow the expansion of movements already seen in the United States and further challenges to the idea of "America" as a cultural entity. These are, of course, debates that have always been a part of the American experience, from the founding period, through the Civil War, to now. But any formative project in the next century will have to consider and account for the power of particular cultural cohesion and cannot easily presume the viability of an American culture that transcends local, ethnic, or racial identities. The church must also prepare for the clashes and conflicts that may emerge from the decline of older, foundational approaches to achieving national cohesion.

The End of Modernity and the Desecularization of the World

Perhaps a more important effect of the demise of modernity and its ideological expressions is the realization that instead of disappearing as anticipated by modern secularists, religion has become a prevalent cultural and political force in the world at the end of the twentieth century. Huntington notes this trend, which began in the 1970s, in his analysis and indicates that all over the world, even in the secular West,

> A new religious approach took shape, aimed no longer at adapting to secular values but at recovering a sacred foundation for the organization of society—by changing society if necessary. Expressed in a multitude of ways, this approach advocated moving on from a modernism that had failed, attributing its setbacks and dead ends to separation from God.[11]

Thus the success of religion, ironically, is attributable in part to the success of modernization, as people seek meaning and community in the midst of the rapid changes and dislocations of the century. Its result, according to Huntington (citing George Weigel), is that "the unsecularization of the world . . . is one of the dominant social facts of the late twentieth century."[12]

John Paul II has noted this development philosophically, referring to "positivism" as the set of prevailing modernist assumptions of the period since the Enlightenment. "Essentially, the positivist mentality, which developed aggressively between the nineteenth and twentieth centuries, is, in a certain sense, fading today. Contemporary man has rediscovered the sacred, even if he does not always know how to identify it."[13] The pope suggests that a global quest for transcendence as fundamental reality in all experience means religion therefore has a renewed and important place in public formation. This openness is a gift to be cultivated by Christians of conviction and commitment to the kingdom of God; it is an opportunity to witness to the truth of the gospel in public life. The already noted opportunities for Christian leadership in cultural formation, due to the relatively high approval of the church in America, may be reinforced by these global trends away from modernity toward other forms of public organization that have significant places for religious belief and cultural association.

Yet this moment is also likely to bring more serious challenges as the effects of the demise of modernity emerge in the United States and the West. James Kurth, commenting on Huntington's clash of civilizations thesis, claims: "At the very moment of its greatest triumph, its defeat of the last great power opposing it, Western civilization is becoming non-Western. . . . The real, and the fatal, reason is that it has become post-modern and therefore post-Western." Kurth challenges the idea of a coherent American and Western world that will stand firm and prevail in the new era. "The real clash of civilizations will not be between the West and the Rest. It will be between the West and the post-West, within the West itself. This clash has already taken place within the brain of Western civilization, the American intellectual class. It is now spreading from that brain to the American body politic."[14] Whether the United States and the West can sustain commitment to transcendent and eternal moorings in the midst of cultural upheaval may be the central question in the "post-positivist" age.

The Loss of Public Meaning

The resurgence of culture and religion as global political forces, as with the widespread religiosity of the American people, should not lead to assumptions of easy public influence by the church. The philosophical developments leading to the decreasing power of modern premises, just as the moral and intellectual ambiguities displayed by Americans in survey research contribute to an environment of uncertainty even as they open up possibilities. In this environment, language alone cannot carry the burden of instruction and formation. Terms that in the past conveyed specific meanings—including public good, leadership, justice, responsibility—can no longer be assumed to have that effect. Richard Rorty argues that in the post-modern era, "the most philosophy can hope to do is to summarize our culturally influenced intuitions about the right thing to do in various situations" rather than pointing to universal, permanent goods uncovered by reason or revealed directly by God.[15] William Grassie claims postmodern beliefs point to ultimate relativism in all experience. This way of thinking

removes all foundational categories by [explaining] them as the causative products of some other factors. There are no available a priori on which to ground human reason, no Archimedean point of reference. . . . There is no direct experience of reality without interpretation; and all interpretation is in some sense corrupted by the cultural and personal prejudices of the interpreter.[16]

Suspicion about meaningful claims was the pervasive attitude in American culture in the last decades of the twentieth century, and it may very well be the case in the new century.

This widespread, powerfully effectual way of looking at life suggests that while "spirituality" may be acceptable, the demand for religious foundations for public life are unlikely to resonate in the absence of commitments "all the way down." No ultimate truth can be experienced or known directly, according to this mind-set; survey data confirm widespread acceptance of this form of relativism. If religious belief is compartmentalized in the way this book demonstrates—with little measurable effect on moral judgments or public decisions—then it is likely that at best a functional use of religion will emerge in the quest for "transcendence." Religion will be used to justify or support what appears to be practically effective. It will be shown that religious people are healthier, more stable, and more committed to public ends. Spirituality will be seen primarily as a means to success, prosperity, and well-being—a more traditional-sounding Transcendental Meditation. For example, one might point to findings that sexual and substance abstinence contributes to physical health and self-esteem, without any sense of their importance to the right order of the soul, to the obligation to respect others, or to the will of God. Likewise, studies may find that stable families produce good workers and stable citizens. The idea of public truth or public authority, or divine norms, will sound quaint and hollow, even as religion becomes an important means of self-development.

These results, however, are not insignificant and may be the best that can be expected in such a pragmatic and pluralistic age. For religion to be taken seriously as a source of insight into practical public good is a step away from its dismissal by scientific rationality. But the results indicate that the richly meaningful concepts that public theologians hope will guide public life will have to be *embodied*—lived out in demonstrable community, not only proclaimed or taught. These concepts must be spread by real people really living them. Thus the church as a complex public order must be realized as the starting point of any hope for formation in the new century.

The Changing Meaning of Law and Virtue

The problem of meaningful language also raises concerns about the possibility of crafting meaningful law. One of the primary contributions of the Jewish-Christian tradition to public life has been the understanding of universal, transcendent law guiding human community.[17] It is the primary responsibility of the government—of the magistrate—to discover and give concrete shape to true law. If having a society that is governed by law implies common understandings of the law and a common basis for adherence to that law, then ambiguity and ambivalence brings this central notion into question in this age. This common core has always been understood to be the essence of a republic, but the corrupted personal and cultural interpretation of all reality indicates that collective obedience to commonly understood, divinely mandated norms is impossible. All that is left is the assertion of power; force and fear are the only common ways of bringing social order. In this view, law is established by the powerful for their own ends. Further, any notion of justice—defining what is the universal good for humans and establishing structures to achieve it—becomes relative and is easily discarded. The venerable concept of confidence in the rule of law, with its biblical origins, is replaced by suspicion and by power conflicts.

A formative project will need to address this atmosphere of suspicion about the real basis of the law. Such a project is likely to face resistance to the ideas that a divine source of law can be reliably known and that humans have obligations to received norms over those they develop on their own. Law in contemporary culture is personalized, to be challenged if it is inconvenient and disobeyed if it interferes with personal happiness. As one survey question put it, "Values are something that each person must decide without being influenced by others"—a sentiment with which a large majority of Americans agreed. This is well put as subjective values have become the key public concept, rather than fixed law or morality. That which is valued by the person doing the valuing, and which is subject to changes in judgment, prevails. We only hope that our values are shared widely enough that order will not have to be too heavily enforced.

This atmosphere may help explain the popularity of public literature that stresses the importance of the cultivation of "virtues" in Americans. William Bennett's *Book of Virtues*[18] and the accompanying video series is the most prominent example of a growing body of works, including those of Robert Fulghum, Robert Coles, and Stephen Covey, that call for a return to personal virtue and responsibility. *In keeping with the current state of public culture, the appeal of "virtues" points in part to the priority in the public mind of personal qualities over a commitment to conformity to norms.* These qualities are valued both for their role in the development of the person and for their instrumental worth in sustaining orderly public life, rather than for reflecting, in the classical sense, an objective right order of soul and society. In this environment, we are left only to hope that the "virtues" cultivated in each person are similar enough to provide some level of common order. This otherwise commendable interest may thus be considered to be in keeping with the trends of postmodern public culture rather than contrary to it; it is the priority of "be all that you can be" over submitting to divine order mediated through earthly institutions.

The rediscovery of virtue as a theme in ethics and education should not be dismissed, and is to be encouraged, when it is approached rightly. Many contributors—Josef Pieper, Peter Kreeft, Stanley Hauerwas, Alisdair MacIntyre, Jean Porter, and J. Budziszewski to name a few—have helped to recover an understanding of virtue as right order in a person conforming to a higher source of order. They have explicated the cardinal and theological virtues and have reconnected the reasoning and actions of the virtuous person with objectively good ends.[19] This understanding contrasts with that of "virtue theorists," who tend to believe that personal qualities understood as virtues are separable from ends and consequences—in effect arguing that intentions and sincerity are all that is necessary to evaluate actions.[20] Michael Slote describes this perspective in *From Morality to Virtue:*

> Those who have spoken of what is or could be distinctive in a genuinely virtue-theoretical approach to ethics, in an ethics in which virtue plays a fundamental, rather than secondary or derivative, role . . . have said that such an ethics will be more interested in the virtuous character of virtuous individuals than in the actions of such individuals, and they have also claimed that virtue ethics should be grounded in aretaic [N.B.: personal excellence] concepts of goodness rather than in deontic notions like "ought," "right," "wrong," and "obligatory."[21]

This situation may provide opportunities as well as challenges, however. While it will not be sufficient for Christians simply to provide a clear articulation of the right norms for human life and community, the endeavor is still necessary. We must clarify what right order of soul and society is and articulate how to depict that order in authoritative constitutional form. This must include a recovery of a public sense of God's created order for humanity, or "natural law," expressed in positive human law. But the demand for personal virtues, while showing that words and constitutions are insufficient in themselves, shows also that formation must acknowledge that humans are not merely impersonal recipients of truth. They must actively know truth and incorporate it into their lives. They must embody knowledge of the law in the practice of civic virtues that indicate consistency and loyalty. Creating Christian community, to show practical and experiential embodiment of the truth, will have public effects as a demonstration of living lawfully and rightly in a cooperative and consensual community that is served by lawful power rather than subservient to arbitrary power. Such a demonstration is critical in a culture that has little sense of what it has in common, a culture that needs to understand that rightly constituted authority is central to its survival and prosperity.

Local Communities of Trust

More and more signs are pointing, then, as this book has been suggesting, to the significance of tangible local expressions of community in the revitalization of common life in the United States. This trend clearly points to a real role for the church as one association remaining *comparatively* viable in American life—though, as noted, its place in public community may also be dropping. As commentators have grappled with many of the problems of cultural change and breakdown that have been explored in this study, many have pointed to the historical significance of local community as a source of moral formation and cultivation of civic virtues in the United States. Jean Bethke Elshtain reminds us that the historical public culture of the United States

> located the child, for example, in his or her little estate, the family, which was itself nested within a wider, overlapping, framework of sustaining and supporting civic institutions: churches, schools, and solidaristic organizations, such as mothers' associations. American society was honeycombed by a vast network that offered a densely textured social ecology for the growing citizen.[22]

She then sums up the current dilemma as derived from the loss of this historical reality:

Curiously, the framers of the American Constitution paid little explicit attention to such institutions, including the family. . . . They simply assumed that these associations of civil society were vital and would be long-lasting. . . . But we no longer can.[23]

Others, sharing the concerns expressed by Elshtain, agree that attention must be paid to the local and tangible forms of community that can nurture citizenship. Americans (and all peoples) still express a preference for particular community—a situation that offers hope for solutions to current dilemmas. Michael Sandel suggests that

it is difficult to imagine a world in which persons were so virtuous that they had no friends, only a universal disposition to friendliness. The problem is not simply that such a world would be difficult to bring about but that it would be difficult to recognize as a human world. The love of humanity is a noble sentiment, but most of the time we live our lives by smaller solidarities. This may reflect certain limits to the bounds of moral sympathy. More important, it reflects the fact that we learn to love humanity not in general but through its particular expressions.[24]

The surveys and other studies cited in this book also show that, even now, to the extent that Americans trust any groups or institutions, they are local ones. As the well-documented decline in confidence in macroinstitutions (national government, media, education, and so on) continues, local institutions retain some level of support, though not overwhelming levels. Comparing responses to questions regarding their feelings about various institutions, Americans on the whole were more inclined to be pleased or enthusiastic about local rather than national expressions.

Table 7.1

Respondents either "pleased with" or "enthusiastic about":

	Local	National
Government	57%	20%
Elected officials	56	18
Economy	59	20
Moral standards	53	17
Schools/education	47	29
Churches	75	57

(Sources: cited surveys)

These responses do not evaluate whether local institutions are under-taking the formative tasks well or successfully. If critics are correct, even local institutions are not performing in the necessary ways, because of their own weaknesses or because of the encroaching power of the national gov-ernment, along with the charted changes in American culture. But the mea-sured significance of the residual levels of trust in local institutions joins the wisdom of many commentators to point to the central role that local institutions must play in civic formation.

The highest level of residual trust remains in *local churches,* again sug-gesting that this perhaps is where formative, or preformative, hope lies. If the moral and intellectual climate in the United States indicates that com-prehensive philosophies of public life, law, and authority cannot now res-onate and guide public life, it may be that the practical wisdom of life in community will be the greatest Christian contribution in the formation of public culture. Public culture continually demonstrates the need for the tangible embodiment of the good life and that abstract statements do not stand alone. So even as they go about their primary task of serving the king-dom of heaven and preparing citizens for it, churches may also cultivate the responsibility and commitment necessary to the formation of temporal public culture. For here is where life is affirmed, human dignity is upheld, true and legitimate authority is revealed, love for others is demonstrated and cultivated, community is experienced, and sacrifice, service, and self-denial are practiced.

The teachings of John Paul II remind us in this regard that we are human *persons,* and as persons, we do not simply receive truth like pictures on a wall, or ideas like words printed on a page. Rather, we experience truth as *active* persons, living it out as well as having ideas about it. This is a fuller and more vital concept of Christian knowing, according to the pope's philo-sophical investigations, than more dispassionate and passive approaches. It indicates that the wisdom that comes from living in community joins with, and is as real as, well-grounded doctrine. Such wisdom includes the aware-ness of transcendent reality as well as the reinforcing effect of experiencing grace and charity in community.

It is urgent to rediscover and to set forth once more the authentic reality of the Christian faith, which is not simply a set of propositions to be accepted with intellectual assent. Rather, faith is a lived knowledge of Christ, a living remembrance of his commandments, and a truth to be lived out. A word, in any event, is not truly received until it passes into action, until it is put into practice. Faith is a decision involving one's whole existence. . . . It entails an act of trusting abandonment to Christ, which enables us to live as he lived (Gal. 2:20), in profound love of God and of our brothers and sisters.[25]

This communitarian concept of public life, known as "personalism," has been powerfully influential in the life of the church in recent years, animating public action in places of oppression such as Eastern Europe and giving force to a tangible understanding of human rights and public life that is fertilizing the soil for commitment to local community among many Christians. This way of seeing can guide American Christians as we ponder our formative role in restoring vibrant public culture in the United States. It points to a full, whole reality, as the Lordship of Christ becomes powerful in all aspects of life, even in public life. It enables an unembarrassed witness of the true good, so that "in every sphere of personal, family, social and political life, morality—founded upon truth and open in truth to authentic freedom—renders a primordial, indispensable and immensely valuable service not only for the individual person and his growth in the good, but also for society and its genuine development."[26]

In facing the challenges of contemporary public culture and the formation of citizens, vibrant Christian communities still have to deal with some "apocalyptic" possibilities that follow from the new realities emerging at the end of the century. Because the state of decline and disarray in American culture may be too far along the road to fragmentation, or because of divine purposes in historical change, we must at least acknowledge that even greater chaos could be ahead. Though the calling may be to formation and preservation, those tasks may take place in radically different circumstances than those we now experience.

The Loss of Public Trust

The question has to be raised whether the current American public and political structure is truly a sustainable experiment. Will the principles of free government and the essential federal republican forms, still so widely supported, remain in place when the culture that has historically sustained them has changed profoundly? Can society be held together in the absence of public trust—which we have documented as declining levels of public confidence, trust in leadership, attachment to the life of the nation, and active citizenship? Francis Fukuyama argues that "people who do not trust one another will end up cooperating only under a system of formal rules and regulations, which have to be negotiated, agreed to, litigated, and enforced, sometimes by coercive means."[27] He believes that public trust has historically been present in American society and has been expressed in the robust economic and civil life that has sustained American culture and has enabled two centuries of relative freedom, limited government, and the development of international power. Furthermore, public trust is found in all robust and prosperous societies.

> Trust is the expectation that arises within a community of regular, honest, and cooperative behavior, based on commonly shared norms, on the part of other members of that community. . . . Social capital is a capability that arises from the prevalence of trust in a society or in certain parts of it. It can be embodied in the smallest and most basic social group, the family, as well as the largest of all groups, the nation, and all other groups in between. . . . The most effective organizations are based on communities of shared ethical values. These communities do not require extensive contract and legal regulation of their relations because prior moral consensus gives members of the group a basis for mutual trust. . . . Acquisition of social capital . . . requires habituation to the moral norms of a community and, in its context, the acquisition of virtues like loyalty, honesty, and dependability. The group, moreover, has to adopt common norms as a whole before trust can become generalized among its members.[28]

Like many analysts, Fukuyama is concerned about the moral and cultural viability of the United States as this social capital of trust declines. This could have devastating economic and political effects, according to his analysis: "Once social capital is spent, it may take centuries to replenish, if it can be replenished at all."[29]

Surveys have confirmed the declining levels of trust among the American public. The Kaiser survey asked, "Would you say that most people can be trusted or that you can't be too careful in dealing with people?" and found that only 35 percent of Americans believed that most of their fellow citizens could be trusted, 63 percent believed that caution is required. The same question asked in a 1964 survey found 54 percent of Americans believed they could trust their fellow citizens. This decline was exceeded by even an greater decline in the level of trust in the federal government: Kaiser surveys have shown that trust in federal government declined from 76 percent in 1964 to 25 percent in 1995.[30] Have we passed the point of replenishment?

Power Shifts

Further, those undertaking the formation of public life must consider whether the pressures of globalization, economic integration, declining national institutions, and the dispersion of sovereignty will change the shape of American public life so drastically as to render its current form no longer viable. Should public philosophy prepare for new forms and new political structures? These structures might be more coercive, with the United States following a path taken by many societies from chaos to dictatorship, with citizens willingly submitting to a strong coercive leader as a remedy to uncertainty and violence. Such a course would have to override the system of divided government and shared powers of the American Constitution. Or they might be some new form of medieval-like corporatism, with diffuse, overlapping, and competing authorities even messier than the current state of American federalism.

In the United States in the late 1990s, many commentators were already pointing to the relative decrease in real power held by elected officials and the rise in power of such bodies as the semiautonomous Federal Reserve Board (which coordinates monetary policy in the United States and, in cooperation with other central banks, around the world) because of the growing centrality of economic factors in social organization. Writing in the May 15, 1997, *New York Times,* James Grant claimed that no political body inspires more reverence or is more powerful than that body:

> The veneration of central banks is the idolatry of the 1990's. Enjoying ultra-low unemployment in the United States, Americans worship and fall down. . . . In this heyday of free markets, central bankers and the currencies they manage have never been more trusted. The stupendous bull market, the apparently endless economic expansion and the historically moderate inflation rate are things of wonder. Well, somebody must have caused them. Somebody, certainly, would be blamed if they went up in smoke. These days, praise or blame seems to fall on one head more than any other, that of the Fed's chairman, Alan Greenspan.[31]

This statement continues to represent the political realities of the early twenty-first century, where not only the Federal Reserve Board but a multitude of agencies, organizations, corporations, and other groups have governing power in America. These groups have gained power but may not have acquired the legitimacy or public support that comes with the development of mechanisms of citizen participation and consent. They may be indifferent or hostile to the norms embodied and cultivated in the Christian community.

Power shifts are also emerging from the oft-noted effects of developments in technology. The machines and instruments of communication and production are more intrusive and pervasive than ever. Our personal tastes and habits are monitored and recorded for multiple public purposes, from marketing to tax collection to traffic control. These advances in technology have had the effect both of freeing Americans from older systems and communities—making them more mobile, less likely to work in factories, and so on—and of tying them into new networks and systems controlled by computers and fiber-optic cables. The effects of technology on individuals and on communities have been studied by many, and we are still grasping the full effects of these revolutions on identity, families, work, politics, religion, and all other areas of life. Responding to the changes in power arrangements that are associated with technological change is among the pressing challenges to any formative project. Whether the new forms of power can be democratic in any sense is a central question. Access to, control of, and response to twenty-first-century technology will be defining factors in political and cultural power arrangements.

Canadian political philosopher George Parkin Grant attempted in *English-Speaking Justice* to convey a picture of an American political system experiencing such shifts in power:

> What can be the place of representative government in the immense society ruled by private and public corporations with their complex bureaucracies? The great founders of our liberalism believed that the best regime required that the choices of all its members should have influence in the governing of the society. It was also hoped that free and equal individuality would be expressed in our work as a field for our choices. . . . How are either of these possible when the dominant decisions come forth from private and public corporations? In this situation, the institutions of representative government seem increasingly to wither in their effectiveness. Lip service is paid to them; but institutions such as elections and parliaments seem to have less and less

constitutive authority. . . . The widespread concentration of most North Americans on private life, and their acceptance that the public realm is something external to them, takes us far away from the original liberal picture of autonomous and equal human beings participating in the government and production of their society.[32]

Rearranging the Boundaries

Is it also possible that a rearrangement of power could open opportunities for forces that would lead to the breakup of the United States? The United States experienced secession and civil war once in its history over deep cultural divisions. As far-fetched as it seems today, breakups were experienced late in the twentieth century by other states—in violent ways, as in Yugoslavia and Ethiopia, and more peacefully, as in the partitions of the USSR and Czechoslovakia. Other seemingly stable states experienced internal pressures from secessionist movements—Spain, Canada, the United Kingdom, China, Russia, among others—in the late 1990s and early in the new century. In 1997 the federal government ended a standoff in Texas with a group that does not recognize the legitimacy of the U.S. annexation of Texas in the 1840s and demands recognition of the "Republic of Texas." Such fringe movements have support only among a very small minority of Americans, but it is possible they indicate the leading edge of something larger. Further, immigration and demographic patterns foreshadow a very different-looking and sounding population by the end of the twenty-first century.

Historically and biblically, no political arrangement should be considered permanent or without potential sources of collapse. The histories of nations and empires demonstrate that even those that seemed well-established and powerful eventually fell or fragmented. The Roman Empire was not eternal, nor was the kingdom of Israel. Seemingly minor weaknesses can quickly grow into fatal infections for a political structure, especially in the absence of public trust, as the leaders of the USSR found out in 1991. Of course, such fragmentary pressure could also stimulate heavy-handed responses, including the use of force and the suspension of civil rights, such as was ordered by Abraham Lincoln in the 1860s to sustain some cohesion during the Civil War. Many current U.S. government scenarios contemplate the possible need for quarantine, emergency powers, and marshal law in the event of terrorist strikes using biological agents or nuclear weapons. Whatever the particular circumstances, it is not out of the question that the United States as we now know it could look very different in a few years—fragmented, or authoritarian, or of course, very much as it looks now.

Hostility and Persecution

Christians must also face the possibility that their beliefs and moral norms will be subject to serious and violent reactions, which may lead to repression. While religious institutions now hold high levels of public support, the widely perceived hostility to religious norms in the public media and the justice system could foreshadow further decline in public faith. The cultural hostility that is troubling to many Christians, with which we began this analysis and which we demonstrated through examination of survey data, could form into more direct expressions of hostility than those already experienced. The window of opportunity for a Christian-led formative project may be small, and may itself provoke responses of greater hostility. Which is, of course, no excuse for inaction; the calling to faithfulness does not depend on the likelihood of success. These realities do call for open-eyed prudence, however, which allows for contingency planning and preparation for what we know is in the range of possible scenarios.

The most prudent course for Christians, in this environment, may be not to take on a constitutional project that pushes major changes in political structure but to continue, in the community life of the church, to work within the current structures and seek to inject them with new meaning. Christendom, after all, was not planned, but grew organically from the soil of hundreds of years of deepening Christian culture. Christians will have a hard time agreeing among themselves about new political forms, and until there is wide consensus that the current "regime" is indeed illegitimate, as some leaders have argued, cultural witness and responsible policy leadership will be most fruitful. But this moment may not last, and more sweeping moves may be just over the horizon. Revolutionary times may not be imminent, but as this study has shown, the storm warnings are becoming ominous. The long tradition of Christian public theology, as well as the promises of ultimate hope given to believers in times of rejection and public turmoil, can provide rich resources for future reconstitution.

Final Thoughts: Eternal Resources

Predictions of cultural conflicts, economic chaos, revolutionary crises, and even unfolding apocalyptic scenarios have proliferated throughout America and the West in recent years, in fiction, film, and popular culture, as well as in extensive analysis. This trend was perhaps brought about by the fascination with the turn of a century and, in this case, the coming of a new millennium. But such predictions surely reflect a widening perception that forces of change, at work in all sectors and levels of society, are leading toward major upheaval. These analyses emanate not only from the disgruntled fringe but from mainstream quarters as well, from theologians to economists, culture analysts, and political leaders.

For example, political analysts William Strauss and Neil Howe (best known for their book *Generations: The History of America's Future*) laid out a detailed scenario for the early twenty-first century in their 1997 release, *The Fourth Turning: An American Prophecy.* Building, in their case, on a theory of generational change, and holding that American history experiences regular cycles of renewal and decline leading to crisis, they argue that we are facing something profound, "sometime around the year 2005, perhaps a few years before or after. . . . A spark will ignite a new mood. Today, the same spark would flame briefly but then extinguish, its last flicker merely confirming and deepening the Unraveling-era mindset. This time, though, it will catalyze a Crisis."[33] The catalyst could be an economic downturn, an election, a foreign crisis, a federal government budget crisis, an AIDS-like plague, a terrorist threat. Perhaps the September 11, 2001, terrorist attacks on the United States will prove to be such a spark. Whatever it is will break open the cultural fragmentation that has been under way for the last twenty-five years or so.

> The new mood and its jarring new problems will provide a natural end point for the Unraveling-era decline in civic confidence. In the pre-Crisis years, fears about the flimsiness of the social contract will have been subliminal but rising. As the Crisis catalyzes, these fears will rush to the surface, jagged and exposed. Distrustful of some things, individuals will feel that their survival requires them to distrust more things. This behavior could cascade into a sudden downward spiral, an implosion of societal trust.
>
> Before long, America's old civic order will seem ruined beyond repair. People will feel like a magnet has passed over society's disk drive, blanking

out the social contract, wiping out old deals, clearing the books of vast unpayable promises to which people had once felt entitled. The economy could reach a trough that may look to be the start of a depression. With American weaknesses newly exposed, foreign dangers could erupt.[34]

Strauss and Howe believe this time of crisis will lead to a temporary, new, more authoritarian order in the United States, which will then give way after the climax of the crisis to a transformed American society. "The emergent society may be something better, a nation that sustains its Framers' visions with a robust new pride. Or it may be something unspeakably worse."[35]

This scenario is representative of many others in its expectation of crisis. But unlike many others, its prescription is essentially to let history take its inevitable course and to prepare for the time of renewal that they hopefully predict. And while in no way built on any Christian insights, it does have a ring of truth for Christians who perceive that larger forces than those marshaled by individuals are at work, that ideas and beliefs have profound consequences, and that ultimate hope rests on faith in things that cannot now be fully seen. Christians, knowing the contrast between temporal, earthly kingdoms, where sin and pestilence corrupt and destroy, and the permanent heavenly kingdom, can face without fear the prospect that crisis is ahead. We know the tentativeness of all human plans and structures.

Other scenarios, of course, present more "optimistic" possibilities. Prosperity, technological development, social progress, and global order are predicted by analysts who anticipate the continuation of the defining characteristics of the comfortable and globalizing post–Cold War decade of the 1990s.

> We are watching the beginnings of a global economic boom on a scale never experienced before. We have entered a period of sustained growth that could eventually double the world's economy every dozen years and bring increasing prosperity for—quite literally—billions of people on the planet. We are riding the early waves of a 25-year run of a greatly expanding economy that will do much to solve seemingly intractable problems like poverty and to ease tensions throughout the world. And we'll do it without blowing the lid off the environment.[36]

Christians can take only partial hope in such developments, however, even if true; such material progress could also come with continued cultural and moral drift and the continued marginalization of the Christian faith as a cultural foundation.

The primary resources the church holds—whether in times of crisis, normalcy, or advancement—are the same as in all ages. They are not primarily in the form of economic, technological, or political power. The resources held by the church can be elaborated in public theology and expressed in effective community life, but they are fundamental to those expressions. Paul's meditations on the three theological virtues remains the best summation of those resources. His hymns to Christian virtue, which we often limit to relationships among Christians or dismiss as sentiments to be sung at weddings, are also our guides to the public and global calling of the church.

Faith points to belief in and trust in the Lord of history, and all that follows from that belief, obeying him in all aspects of life, including public life.

Hope is knowing that he is Lord and that he will ultimately guide all things in conformity to his will, even if immediate experiences are crushing.

Love is the power to serve in his name, in the church and in the world as he does.

These theological virtues point our attention to Christ, who remains when all else fails. Even if nations crumble and cultures fall into disarray, his kingdom is forever. And he has always been faithful to sustain the church, the bearer of these virtues and the guardian of the truth, through all generations and civilizations.

The church has faced cultural decline in many times and places. These times of crisis have sometimes been periods of ferment and reflection even as the world around crumbles, such as when Augustine faced the collapse of Rome and the apparent failure of civilization by producing the most profound works of theology and public philosophy. All times have their own forms of power and opposition; all are hostile in some degree to faith and Christian norms. Thus all times need to be discerned and faced with the primary resources available to the church.

The greatest lesson of all of these experiences is that the church never fully knows the meaning of its current situation or the shape of the future;

it never has full insight into the intentions of the Lord. Nor do we have any magic means of accurately knowing the immediate future. These are times, though, in which the practice of faith, holding trust in him who is worthy of trust, is the most important calling. Faith results in faithfulness, faithfulness to the calling of love for the culture and the world. By attentive cultivation of its holy life together, in robust communities of faith where understanding is formed, the church will offer its greatest contribution to the shaping of culture toward right and just order. If American culture continues to resist such prophetic demonstration, or even if it responds with acceptance and repentance, our faith tells us that all is still under the judgment of God and subject to his purposes.

We might ask, in light of all this evidence, what is it that holds the United States together now? Why have these forces not already brought about the fragmentation they indicate? Are we joining the Cassandra chorus that, as in the past, is still wrong about America when we call attention to these indicators? The fact that the United States still holds together somehow perhaps indicates that the capability in American culture to respond to challenges with pragmatic fixes will win even in the new situation of advanced moral and cultural pluralism.

However, the evidence from this study points in a different direction. The measurable residual strength still to be found in the local church emerges as the primary factor in offering the salt of preservation—even with the weakening effects of the erosion of religion in society. To continue such preservation in an increasingly fragmentary culture, the church will need to remain true to its calling and its faith as it serves its ultimate hope. Such faithfulness will be the crucible both of public virtue and of public leadership.

Notes

Introduction

1. Richard Mouw, "Religious Conviction and Public Civility," in *Ethics, Religion, and the Good Society*, ed. Joseph Runzo (Louisville: Westminster/John Knox, 1992), 95–107.

2. See, for example, Arne Rasmussen, *The Church as Polis* (Notre Dame, Ind.: University of Notre Dame Press, 1994) and D. Stephen Long, *Divine Economy* (London and New York: Routledge, 2000).

3. Valerie Strauss, "Philosophy's Resurgence," *Washington Post*, 31 October 2000, A11.

4. Paul Gigot, "Two Countries, One System," *Wall Street Journal*, 9 November 2000.

5. Tony Blankley, "Democracy in Peril," *Washington Times*, 15 November 2000.

6. Andrew Sullivan, "Gore Plots Next Step in Legal Coup," *Sunday Times (London)*, 26 November 2000.

7. For helpful insight on this point, see James S. Taylor, *Poetic Knowledge* (Albany, N.Y.: State University of New York Press, 1998); and Marion Montgomery, *The Reflective Journey toward Order: Essays on Dante, Wordsworth, Eliot and Others* (Athens: University of Georgia Press, 1973) and *Possum, and Other Receipts for the Recovery of "Southern" Being* (Athens: University of Georgia Press, 1987).

8. Lesslie Newbigin, *The Gospel in a Pluralist Society* (Grand Rapids: Eerdmans; and Geneva: WCC Publications, 1989).

9. Oliver O'Donovan, *The Desire of Nations: Rediscovering the Roots of Political Theology* (Cambridge: Cambridge University Press, 1996), 42.

Chapter 1: *Christian Resources for Public Life in the Twenty-First Century*

1. Max Stackhouse, "A Premature Postmodern," *First Things* 106 (October 2000): 21.

2. Oliver O'Donovan, *The Desire of Nations*, 82.

3. James Davison Hunter, *Culture Wars: The Struggle to Define America* (New York: Basic, 1991), 53.

4. Roger Lundin, *The Culture of Interpretation: Christian Faith and the Postmodern World* (Grand Rapids: Eerdmans, 1993), 4.

5. See John Paul II, *Evangelium Vitae*, 1995.

6. John Paul II, *Centesimus Annus*, section 24 (Editions Paulines, 1991), 44.

7. James Davison Hunter and Carl Bowman, *The State of Disunion: The 1996 Survey of American Political Culture,* vol. 1, *Summary Report,* and vol. 2, *Summary Tables* (Charlottesville, Va.: *In Medias Res* Educational Foundation, 1996).

8. George Lakoff, *Moral Politics: What Conservatives Know That Liberals Don't* (Chicago and London: University of Chicago Press, 1996), 3.

9. Michael J. Sandel, *Democracy's Discontent: America in Search of a Public Philosophy* (Cambridge, Mass. and London: Belknap, 1996), 4.

10. Ibid., 24.

11. Ibid., 317.

12. Ibid., 321.

13. Ibid., 347.

14. Ibid., 351.

15. Richard Rorty in Gordon D. Marino, "Shattering Philosophy's Mirror: A Conversation with Richard Rorty," *Commonweal* 121, no. 9 (6 May 1994): 11.

16. Keith Topper, "Richard Rorty, Liberalism and the Politics of Redescription," *American Political Science Review* 89, no. 4 (1995): 954.

17. Richard Rorty, *Consequences of Pragmatism* (Minneapolis: University of Minnesota Press, 1983), 166.

18. *Centesimus Annus,* section 13 (Editions Paulines), 27.

19. Ernst Troeltsch, *The Social Teaching of the Christian Churches* (Louisville: Westminster/John Knox, 1992 reprint).

20. O'Donovan, *The Desire of Nations,* 1.

21. Ibid., 2.

22. John Milbank, *Theology and Social Theory: Beyond Secular Reason* (Oxford: Blackwell, 1991), 380.

23. Ibid.

24. See, for example, Richard J. Mouw, *When the Saints Come Marching In* (Grand Rapids: Eerdmans, 1983); Albert M. Wolters, *Creation Regained: Biblical Basics for a Reformational Worldview* (Grand Rapids: Eerdmans, 1985); and Oliver O'Donovan, *Resurrection and Moral Order: An Outline for Evangelical Ethics* (Leicester, England: InterVarsity Press, 1986).

25. Augustine, *City of God* (trans. Marcus Dods), 5.11.

Chapter 2: *The Historical Context*

1. T. S. Eliot, "The Idea of a Christian Society," in *Christianity and Culture* (New York: Harcourt Brace, 1960), 9.

2. John Winthrop, "A Model of Christian Charity," in *The Winthrop Papers* (Boston: Massachusetts Historical Society, 1931), 282–95.

3. Eliot, "Idea of a Christian Society," 41.

4. Joan Lockwood O'Donovan, *Theology of Law and Authority in the English Reformation* (Atlanta: Scholars, 1991), 1.

5. Ibid., 160.

6. Hubert Box, *The Principles of Canon Law* (London: Oxford University Press, 1949), 8.

7. American Articles of Religion, art. 37.

8. John Adams, "A Dissertation on the Canon and Feudal Law," in *Political Writings,* ed. Charles Peek (New York: Liberal Arts Press, 1953), 6.

9. Ibid., 9.

10. These quotations in this and the next paragraph are from the *BCP,* 1928 American version, but they are also to be found in other versions of the prayer book prior to that of 1979, and are the compositions of Thomas Cranmer.

11. *Book of Common Prayer* 1928, 32.

12. *The Constitutions and Canons Ecclesiastical Made in the Year 1603* (London: SPCK, 1960), 2.

13. John Henry Blunt, *The Book of Church Law,* 10th ed. (London: Longmans, Green and Co., 1905), 5–7.

14. Ibid., 8.

15. John Calvin, *Institutes of the Christian Religion,* 4.20.1.

16. Ibid., 4.20.2.

17. Ibid., 4.20.3.

18. Eliot, "Idea of a Christian Society," 27.

19. James S. Taylor, *Poetic Knowledge* (Albany: State University of New York Press, 1998), 35.

20. Ibid., 5.

21. C. S. Lewis, *The Discarded Image* (Cambridge: Cambridge University Press, 1964), 12.

22. Charles Taylor, *Sources of the Self* (Cambridge: Harvard University Press, 1989), 287.

23. Robert Louis Wilken, "In Defense of Constantine," *First Things* 112 (April 2001): 36.

24. For elaboration of the anti-Constantiniaism perspective, see Arne Rasmussen's discussion in *The Church as Polis: From Political Theology to Theological Politics as Exemplified by Jurgen Moltmann and Stanley Hauerwas* (Lund, Sweden: Lund University Press, 1994), 78ff.

25. Wilken, "In Defense of Constantine," 36.

26. Jean Porter, *Natural and Divine Law* (Grand Rapids: Eerdmans, 1999), 126.

27. For a detailed discussion, see J. Budziszewski, *Written on the Heart: The Case for Natural Law* (Downers Grove, Ill.: InterVarsity Press, 1997), 86–99.

28. Roger Williams, "The Bloody Tenent of Persecution," [1644] from *A More Perfect Union: Documents in U.S. History,* eds. Paul F. Boller and Ronald Story (New York: Houghton Mifflin, 1984).

29. See, for example: George Washington's *Farewell Address,* and the excellent survey by Thomas West, "Religious Liberty: The View from the Founding," in Daniel Palm, *On Faith and Free Government* (New York: Rowan and Littlefield, 1997), 3ff.

30. See Os Guinness, *The Great Experiment: Faith and Freedom in America* (Colorado Springs: Navpress, 2001).

31. Gottlieb Mittelberger, "Journey to Pennsylvania in the Year 1750 and Return to Germany in the Year 1754," in *Documents of Modern History: English Colonization of North America,* eds. Louis B. Wright and Elaine W. Fowler (New York: St. Martin's, 1967), 103.

32. John Jay, *The Federalist Papers #2,* ed. Clinton Rossiter (New York: Penguin, 1961), 38.

33. Edmund Burke, "Speech on Moving His Resolutions for Conciliation with the Colonies," March 22, 1775, in *Burke's Speeches,* ed. F. G. Selby (Westport, Conn.: Greenwood, 1974), 80.

34. Ibid., 82.

35. Taylor, *Sources of the Self,* 274.

36. Ibid., 279.

184   Notes

37. Burke, "Speech for Conciliation with the Colonies," 80.
38. Ibid.
39. Taylor, *Sources of the Self,* 285.
40. Vigen Guroian, *Ethics After Christendom* (Grand Rapids: Eerdmans, 1994), 12.

Chapter 3: *The Search for a Common Public Philosophy in America*

1. Data employed in developing this chapter are drawn from the following: James Davison Hunter and Carl Bowman, *The State of Disunion: The 1996 Survey of American Political Culture,* 2 vols. (Charlottesville, Va.: *In Medias Res* Foundation, 1996); the *Washington Post*/Kaiser Family Foundation/Harvard University survey project, "Why Don't Americans Trust the Government?" (1996); The NPR/Kaiser Family Foundation/Kennedy School Poll 2000, "Attitudes toward Government" (Menlo Park, Calif.: Henry J. Kaiser Family Foundation); the *Washington Post*/Kaiser Family Foundation/Harvard University survey, "Issues in the 2000 Election: Values," (2000); 1996 and 2000 national election studies from the University of Michigan; "Giving and Volunteering in the United States" (New York: Independent Sector, 1992); and other small surveys as noted.
2. Hunter and Bowman, *The 1996 Survey.*
3. Robert Putnam, *Bowling Alone: The Collapse and Revival of American Community* (New York: Simon and Schuster, 2000); "Bowling Alone: America's Declining Social Capital," *Journal of Democracy* (January 1995).
4. Charles Taylor, *The Malaise of Modernity* (Concord, Ontario: House of Anansi, 1991), 117.
5. Jean Bethke Elshtain, *Democracy on Trial* (New York: Basic, 1995), 24–25.
6. Ibid., 31.

Chapter 4: *The Search for Common Identity, Morality, and Political Goals*

1. Alexis de Tocqueville, *Democracy in America,* 1.2.9 (New York: Anchor, 1969), 294.
2. From *The Survey of American Political Culture* and Gallup surveys on religious belief.
3. Tocqueville, *Democracy in America,* 538.
4. "Issue Referendum Reveals Mix of Liberal and Conservative Views in America Today," The Gallup Organization, November 1, 2000.
5. Independent Sector survey, "Giving and Volunteering in the United States," 1992.

Chapter 5: *Christian Public Philosophy and Theology at the Beginning of the Twenty-First Century*

1. See Ashley Woodiwiss, "Do We Really Need a Public Philosophy?" *Books and Culture* (January/February 1997): 28–29.
2. Letter from Don Eberly to participants, November 25, 1996. Meeting held January 10, 1997, Washington, D.C.
3. James W. Skillen, *Recharging the American Experiment* (Grand Rapids: Baker, 1994), 165.
4. Barry Harvey, "Insanity, Theocracy, and the Public Realm: Public Theology, the Church, and the Politics of Liberal Democracy" *Modern Theology* 10, no. 1 (January 1994): 46.
5. Ashley Woodiwiss, "Going Votin' or Going Fishin'?" *Regeneration Quarterly* 2, no. 3 (summer 1996): 12.
6. Harvey, "Insanity, Theocracy, and the Public Realm," 50.

7. Ibid., 51.

8. Don Eberly, "From Cultural Protest to Cultural Recovery," *Regeneration Quarterly* 2, no. 3, (summer 1996): 27.

9. National Association of Evangelicals, NAE Washington Insight, March 1993.

10. "Leaders of the Christian Right Announce Their Next Step," *Christianity Today*, 13 December 1985, 65.

11. Doug Bandow, *Beyond Good Intentions: A Biblical View of Politics* (Westchester, Ill: Crossway, 1988), 104.

12. Jim Wallis, *The Soul of Politics: A Practical and Prophetic Vision for Change* (New York: The New Press; Maryknoll, N.Y.: Orbis, 1994), 4.

13. Richard John Neuhaus, *The Naked Public Square,* 2d ed. (Grand Rapids: Eerdmans, 1986), 141.

14. George Weigel, *Soul of the World: Notes on the Future of Public Catholicism* (Grand Rapids: Eerdmans, 1996), 6.

15. Paul Marshall, "Politics Not Ethics: A Christian Perspective on the State" (Toronto: Institute for Christian Studies, 1986). See also Paul Marshall, *Thine Is the Kingdom: A Biblical Perspective on the Nature of Government and Politics Today* (Grand Rapids: Eerdmans, 1984).

16. Oliver O'Donovan, *The Desire of Nations: Rediscovering the Roots of Political Theology* (Cambridge: Cambridge University Press, 1996), 3.

17. See Amy L. Sherman, *Preferential Option: A Christian and Neoliberal Strategy for Latin America's Poor* (Grand Rapids: Eerdmans, 1992); Herbert Schlossberg, Vinay Samuel, and Ronald J. Sider, *Christianity and Economics in the Post–Cold War Era* (Grand Rapids: Eerdmans, 1994); Craig M. Gay, *With Liberty and Justice for Whom?* (Grand Rapids: Eerdmans, 1991); Richard John Neuhaus, *Doing Well and Doing Good: The Challenge to the Christian Capitalist,* (New York: Doubleday, 1992); D. Stephen Long, *Divine Economy,* (London and New York: Routledge, 2000).

18. Ralph Reed Jr., "What Religious Conservatives Want," in *Disciples and Democracy,* ed. Michael Cromartie (Grand Rapids: Eerdmans, 1994), 7.

19. Paul M. Weyrich, "Separate and Free," *Washington Post,* 7 March 1999, B7; and Cal Thomas and Ed Dobson, *Blinded by Might: Can the Religious Right Save America?* (Grand Rapids: Zondervan, 1999). See also Thomas Edsall, "Key Conservative Surrenders in Culture War, but Fight Continues," *Washington Post,* 18 February 1999, A6.

20. George Parkin Grant, *Technology and Justice* (Notre Dame, Ind.: University of Notre Dame Press, 1986), 118.

21. O'Donovan, *The Desire of Nations,* 20.

22. Ibid., 231.

23. C. S. Lewis, "Membership," in *The Weight of Glory and Other Addresses* (Grand Rapids: Eerdmans, 1965), 36.

24. Reinhold Niebuhr, *The Children of Light and the Children of Darkness* (New York: Charles Scribners Sons, 1944), xiii.

25. Weigel, *Soul of the World,* 147.

26. Ibid., 40.

27. Tage Lindblom, *The Myth of Democracy* (Grand Rapids: Eerdmans, 1996), 54.

28. For an overview of the "principled pluralism" perspective in both its Catholic and Reformational expressions, see James W. Skillen and Rockne M. McCarthy, *Political Order and the Plural Structure of Society* (Atlanta: Scholars, 1991).

29. Luis Lugo, "Caesar's Coin and the Politics of the Kingdom: A Pluralist Perspective," in *Caesar's Coin: Christians and the Limits of Government* (Washington: Ethics and Public Policy Center; Grand Rapids: Eerdmans, 1996), 12.

30. Max L. Stackhouse, *Public Theology and Political Economy: Christian Stewardship in Modern Society* (Grand Rapids: Eerdmans, 1987), 163.

31. Richard J. Mouw and Sander Griffioen, *Pluralism and Horizons: An Essay in Christian Public Philosophy* (Grand Rapids: Eerdmans, 1993), 128.

32. Ronald F. Thiemann, *Constructing a Public Theology: The Church in a Pluralistic Culture* (Louisville: Westminster/John Knox, 1991), 119.

33. Richard John Neuhaus, "The End of Democracy? The Judicial Usurpation of Politics," *First Things* 67 (November 1996): 19.

34. Ibid.

35. Charles W. Colson, "Kingdoms in Conflict," *First Things* 67 (November 1996): 37.

36. William J. Bennett, "The End of Democracy? A Discussion Continued," *First Things* 69 (January 1997): 19.

37. James C. Dobson, "The End of Democracy? A Discussion Continued," *First Things* 69 (January 1997): 21.

38. Richard M. Weaver, *The Southern Tradition at Bay: A History of Postbellum Thought* (New Rochelle, N.Y.: Arlington House, 1968), 376.

39. Calvin DeWitt, *The Environment and the Christian: What Can We Learn from the New Testament?* (Grand Rapids: Baker, 1991), 115.

40. Ian Bradley, *God Is Green: Ecology for Christians* (New York: Doubleday, 1990), 11.

41. Douglas John Hall, *The Steward: A Biblical Symbol Come of Age* (Grand Rapids: Eerdmans, 1990), 130–32.

42. Thiemann, *Constructing a Public Theology,* 43.

Chapter 6: *Church-Shaping Culture and Culture-Shaping Church*

1. In addition to the surveys already cited, see for comparison, George Barna and Mark Hatch, *Boiling Point* (Ventura, Calif.: Regal, 2001).

2. Henry G. Brinton, "Our Church Offers God, Counseling, Free Parking . . . ," *Washington Post*, 11 May 1997, C3.

3. Ibid.

4. Robert Putnam, *Bowling Alone: The Collapse and Revival of American Community* (New York: Simon and Schuster, 2000), 78.

5. Robin Gill, *Churchgoing and Christian Ethics* (Cambridge: Cambridge University Press, 1999), 5.

6. Robert Putnam, *Bowling Alone,* 67.

7. David Myers, *The American Paradox: Spiritual Hunger in an Age of Paradox* (New Haven: Yale University Press, 2000), 112.

Chapter 7: *Obstacles and Opportunities for Christians in the Twenty-First Century*

1. Michael Walzer, "Between Nation and World," *The Economist,* 11 September 1993, 49.

2. Michael Sandel, *Democracy's Discontent: America in Search of a Public Philosophy* (Cambridge, Mass. and London: Belknap, 1986), 351.

3. Oliver O'Donovan, *The Desire of Nations: Rediscovering the Roots of Political Theology* (Cambridge: Cambridge University Press, 1996), 72.

4. See, for example, Henry Kissinger, *Diplomacy* (New York: Simon and Schuster, 1994); John Lewis Gaddis, *The United States and the End of the Cold War: Implications, Reconsiderations, Provocations* (New York: Oxford University Press, 1992) and *We Now Know: Rethinking Cold War History* (New York: Oxford University Press, 1997); Seyom Brown, *New Forces, Old Forces and the Future of World Politics*, post–Cold War edition (New York: HarperCollins, 1995); and Francis Fukuyama, *The End of History and the Last Man* (London: Penguin, 1992).

5. Richard Rorty, "Human Rights, Rationality and Sentimentality," *Yale Review* 81, no. 4 (October 1994): 4.

6. Samuel P. Huntington, *The Clash of Civilizations and the Remaking of World Order* (New York: Simon and Schuster, 1996), 21.

7. Ibid., 41.

8. Ibid., 28.

9. In the United States, arguments for proportional representation (PR) come in at least two forms. The first calls for ensuring adequate racial and ethnic minority representation in legislative bodies through creating districts where minority groups hold the majority of votes. The second form is in line with the standard definition of PR as practiced in most parliamentary democracies: it calls for adoption of some system of distributing legislative seats to political parties according to the proportion of votes received, allowing for the formation of multiple parties. See, for example, the arguments of James Skillen in *Recharging the American Experiment: Principled Pluralism for Genuine Civic Community* (Grand Rapids: Baker, 1994), 137–56; Michael Lind, "A Radical Plan to Change American Politics," *Atlantic Monthly*, August 1992, 73–83; Douglas Amy, *Real Choices/New Voices: The Case for Proportional Representation Elections in the United States* (New York: Columbia University Press, 1993); Nick Loenen, *Citizenship and Democracy: A Case for Proportional Representation* (Toronto: Dundum, 1997); also consult documents available from the Center for Voting and Democracy, <www.igc.apc.org/cvd>.

10. Wendell Berry, *What Are People For?* (New York: Northpoint, 1990), 8.

11. Huntington, *The Clash of Civilizations*, 96.

12. Ibid.

13. John Paul II, *Crossing the Threshold of Hope* (New York: Alfred A. Knopf, 1995), 32.

14. James Kurth, "The Real Clash," *The National Interest* 37 (fall 1994): 14.

15. Rorty, "Human Rights, Rationality and Sentimentality," 5.

16. William Grassie, "Postmodernism: What One Needs to Know," *Zygon* 32, no. 1 (March 1997): 86.

17. See Joan Lockwood O'Donovan, *Theology of Law and Authority in the English Reformation* (Atlanta: Scholars Press, 1991); J. Budziszewski, *Written on the Heart: The Case for Natural Law* (Downers Grove, Ill.: InterVarsity Press, 1997); Jean Porter, *Natural and Divine Law: Reclaiming the Tradition for Christian Ethics* (Grand Rapids: Eerdmans, 1999).

18. William J. Bennett, *The Book of Virtues* (New York: Simon and Schuster, 1993).

19. For the definitive study of the classical and Christian understanding of the virtues, see Josef Pieper, *The Four Cardinal Virtues* (Notre Dame, Ind.: University of Notre Dame Press, 1966). See also Peter Kreeft, *Back to Virtue: Traditional Moral Wisdom for Modern Moral Confusion* (Harrison, N.Y.: Ignatius Press, 1992); Alisdair MacIntyre, *After Virtue: A Study in Moral Theory*, 2d ed. (Notre Dame, Ind.: University of Notre Dame Press, 1984); Stanley Hauerwas, *Vision and Virtue: Essays in Christian Ethical Reflection* (Notre Dame, Ind.: Fides Publishers, 1975); Jean Porter, *Moral Action and Christian Ethics* (Cambridge: Cambridge University Press,

1995), and *Natural and Divine Law* (Cambridge: Cambridge University Press, 1995); J. Budziszewski, *Written on the Heart*; John Finnis, *Fundamentals of Ethics* (Washington, D.C.: Georgetown University Press, 1983); Kenneth Kirk, *Some Principles of Moral Theology* (London: Longmans, Green and Co., 1930); R. C. Mortimer, *The Elements of Moral Theology* (London: Adam and Charles Black, 1947); H. R. McAdoo, *The Structure of Caroline Moral Theology* (London: Longmans, Green and Co., 1948).

20. See the essays in Roger Crisp and Michael Slote, eds. *Virtue Ethics* (Oxford: Oxford University Press, 1997), especially the essay by Michael Slote, "Agent-Based Virtue Ethics," 234–62. See also in this volume the 1958 essay by G. E. M. Anscombe, "Modern Moral Philosophy," 26–44, considered to be the opening bell in the reawakening of interest in virtue in the twentieth century, in which she contrasts the significance of law with utilitarianism and other perspectives.

21. Michael Slote, *From Morality to Virtue* (Oxford: Oxford University Press, 1992), xiv.

22. Jean Bethke Elshtain, *Democracy on Trial* (New York: Basic, 1995), 6.

23. Ibid.

24. Michael J. Sandel, *Democracy's Discontent: America in Search of a Public Philosophy* (Cambridge, Mass. and London: Belknap), 342.

25. John Paul II, *Veritatis Splendor* (1993), no. 88.

26. Ibid., no. 101.

27. Francis Fukuyama, *Trust: The Social Virtues and the Creation of Prosperity* (New York: Free Press, 1995), 27.

28. Ibid., 26.

29. Ibid., 321.

30. The *Washington Post*/ Kaiser Family Foundation/ Harvard University Survey Project, "Why Don't Americans Trust The Government?" (Menlo Park, Calif.: Henry J. Kaiser Family Foundation, 1996).

31. James Grant, "Demigods in Pinstripes," *New York Times,* 15 May 1997.

32. George Parkin Grant, *English-Speaking Justice* (Notre Dame, Ind.: University of Notre Dame Press, 1986), 10. See also Albert H. Teich, ed., *Technology and the Future*, 6th ed. (New York: St. Martin's, 1993) for a helpful collection of varying perspectives on technology; and Albert Borgmann, *Technology and the Character of Contemporary Life: A Philosophical Inquiry* (Chicago: University of Chicago Press, 1984). Many Christians have also been guided in their thinking about technology by the works of Jacques Ellul, notably *The Technological Society* (New York: Seabury, 1964) and *The Presence of the Kingdom* (New York: Seabury, 1967).

33. William Strauss and Neil Howe, *The Fourth Turning: An American Prophecy* (New York: Broadway, 1997), 272.

34. Ibid., 274–75.

35. Ibid., 278.

36. See Peter Schwartz and Peter Leyden, "The Long Boom: A History of the Future 1980–2020," *Wired,* July 1997: 116.

Subject Index